Raise Her Up

Stories AND *Lessons* FROM *Women* IN *International Educational Leadership*

DEBRA E. LANE & KIMBERLY CULLEN

ELSA DONOHUE • SUZETTE JULIEN • MICHELLE KUHNS • KATE McKENNA

ALEASHA MORRIS • FRANCESCA MULAZZI • MAYA NELSON • PAULINE O'BRIEN

FOREWORD BY JOELLEN KILLION

Solution Tree | Press

a division of

Solution Tree

555 North Morton Street
Bloomington, IN 47404
800.733.6786 (toll free) / 812.336.7700
FAX: 812.336.7790

email: info@SolutionTree.com
SolutionTree.com

Visit **go.SolutionTree.com/leadership** to download the free reproducibles in this book.

Printed in the United States of America

Library of Congress Cataloging-in-Publication Data

Names: Lane, Debra E., author. | Cullen, Kimberly, author.
Title: Raise her up : stories and lessons from women in international
   educational leadership / Debra E. Lane, Kimberly Cullen.
Description: Bloomington, IN : Solution Tree Press, [2022] | Includes
   bibliographical references and index.
Identifiers: LCCN 2021061489 (print) | LCCN 2021061490 (ebook) | ISBN
   9781952812996 (paperback) | ISBN 9781949539578 (ebook)
Subjects: LCSH: Women school administrators--Case studies. | Women school
   administrators--Anecdotes. | Women in education--Case studies. |
   Educational leadership--Case studies. | International
   schools--Administration--Case studies.
Classification: LCC LB2831.82 .L36 2022 (print) | LCC LB2831.82 (ebook) |
   DDC 371.20082--dc23/eng/20220215
LC record available at https://lccn.loc.gov/2021061489
LC ebook record available at https://lccn.loc.gov/2021061490

Solution Tree
Jeffrey C. Jones, CEO
Edmund M. Ackerman, President

Solution Tree Press
President and Publisher: Douglas M. Rife
Associate Publisher: Sarah Payne-Mills
Managing Production Editor: Kendra Slayton
Editorial Director: Todd Brakke
Art Director: Rian Anderson
Copy Chief: Jessi Finn
Production Editor: Paige Duke
Content Development Specialist: Amy Rubenstein
Acquisitions Editor: Sarah Jubar
Proofreader: Elisabeth Abrams
Text and Cover Designer: Abigail Bowen
Editorial Assistants: Charlotte Jones, Sarah Ludwig, and Elijah Oates

The cover artwork comes from a botanical composition made with colored pencils, flowers, and leaves, created in 2021 by artist Japinest to commemorate International Women's Day and celebrate rapport among women. Visit www.japinest.com to learn more about the artist.

Acknowledgments

We are profoundly grateful to Douglas Rife, president of Solution Tree Press, who encouraged us to follow our instincts on this book, recognizing that the stories of women leaders and the barriers they encounter need to be shared.

Special thanks to Claudia Wheatley and Amy Rubenstein, who believed in our potential as storytellers and who pushed us to be better writers.

To Mikel Tribe: a thousand thanks for being our first full reader and giving us thorough and thoughtful feedback.

We are eternally thankful to the women whose stories are highlighted in this book, and for their bravery, vulnerability, and unwavering support of the project.

To Joellen Killion, whose powerful foreword gave us the final push we needed on that first draft.

We thank our children—Alex, Miles, Liam, Cullen, Ignacio, Emma, Eefje, and Marco—who are the main reasons we do the work we do. While it will ultimately be up to them to make the world a more equal, equitable place for all, we hope that our work will make things at least a little better. We trust they will never settle for less than they deserve and will leave the world a better place than it was when they got here.

To Pauline O'Brien, we thank you for recognizing synergy and bringing us together. To Beth P., Bridget M., Anne Marie L., Marsha L., Jeannine R., Judy C., Leslie R., Vickie A., and all of the amazing women in our lives who may not make an appearance in this book but whose stories inspire us daily: we see you, we appreciate you, we are you. Raise her up!

Solution Tree Press would like to thank the following reviewers:

Jennifer Abrams
Consultant
Palo Alto, California

Heather Bell-Williams
Principal, Milltown Elementary School
Anglophone South School District
St. Stephen, New Brunswick, Canada

Molly Capps
Principal
McDeeds Creek Elementary
Southern Pines, North Carolina

Lorrie Hulbert
Principal
Floyd L. Bell Elementary School
Kirkwood, New York

Nicole McRee
Science Instructional Coach
Kildeer Countryside District 96
Buffalo Grove, Illinois

Sarah Stobaugh
Principal
Morrilton Intermediate
Morrilton, Arkansas

Tracey Vander Hayden
Principal
Pioneer Middle School
Tustin, California

Dawn Vang
Assistant Principal
McDeeds Creek Elementary
Southern Pines, North Carolina

Visit **go.SolutionTree.com/leadership** to download the free reproducibles in this book.

Table of Contents

About the Authors

Debra E. Lane, EdD, has been an educator for more than thirty years, as a teacher and administrator in the United States and abroad. She has led several schools as principal, including Shanghai American School, one of the world's leading international schools. She has taught grades from pre-K through middle school, as well as ESOL, literacy, and gifted and talented classes in Fairfax County Public Schools and in the Dominican Republic. In 2020, she was director of talent development at Alexandria City Public Schools.

Debra's dissertation work on bullying prevention led her to act as advisor and consultant for government agencies, associations, and school boards on effective bullying prevention strategies both locally and internationally. She has taught undergraduate and graduate classes at George Mason University and the University of Virginia. As part of her work with the National Staff Development Council, she applied current research in adult learning to her work on staff development, focusing on professional learning communities. She has presented at numerous international conferences, including Near East South Asia Council of Overseas Schools, Tri-Association, National Council of Teachers of Mathematics, Learning Forward, and through her work with the Chesapeake Bay Foundation and the National Science Foundation.

Debra is working on federal government grants focusing on transformative leadership and increasing teachers' leadership and instructional roles across the United States and Central and South America. She has also participated in accreditation teams in China and Hong Kong with the Western Association of Schools and Colleges. She was nominated as Virginia Principal of the Year and won the Chesapeake Bay Foundation Educator of the Year Award in 2009. Debra is also an educational consultant at Lane Leadership Group, LLC. She serves as a board member with NoVA Outside, GrandInvolve, Virginia Association for Environmental Education, Fall for the Book literary festival at George Mason University, George Mason University Curriculum Advisory Council, and IDEA (Inclusive Development Education for Adolescents).

Debra holds a bachelor of science from Baylor University, master's degrees from Virginia Tech and George Mason University, and a doctorate in education from the University of Virginia.

To learn more about Debra Lane's work, follow @LaneDebra on Twitter.

To book Debra E. Lane for professional development, contact pd@SolutionTree.com.

Kimberly Cullen, an American citizen born in Brazil and raised in Texas and Spain, is an adult third-culture kid who understands the unique benefits and opportunities that come from having cross-cultural experiences during the developmental years. Kimberly worked for twenty-three years in an international school based in Madrid, Spain, where she held a variety of roles including head of development and community liaison, guidance and college counselor, dean of students, secondary teacher, and upper school director. Additionally, Kimberly served as the internal coordinator for accreditation for over fifteen years and has participated in accreditation site visits for Middle States Association of Colleges and Schools.

Kimberly has served the international and independent K–12 school communities as a professional coach and consultant. She is one of the founding members of the International Collaborative for Coaching Professionals, and she has led professional development for international educators around leadership and coaching. Additionally, Kimberly serves on the board of directors of the Music for Healing and Transition Program, a nonprofit educational organization that trains musicians to provide therapeutic music to those in need.

Kimberly has a master of arts in education with a specialization in education of the hearing-impaired from the University of Hertfordshire in the United Kingdom, a master of science in human services with a specialization in counseling studies from Capella University, and a bachelor of arts in religious studies from Hamilton College.

To learn more about Kimberly Cullen's work, visit www.kimberlycullen.com and follow @cullenkim on Twitter.

To book Kimberly Cullen for professional development, contact pd@SolutionTree.com.

About the Contributors

Elsa Donohue has taught, led, and learned in nine different countries. Elsa is the head of school at Vientiane International School (VIS) in Vientiane, Laos. Before moving to Laos in 2018, she was the principal of the two campuses of the elementary division at Jakarta Intercultural School (JIS) in Indonesia. Her devotion to teaching and learning has led her to inquire continuously into what constitutes a quality experience for all learners (from age three to adulthood). After attaining a bachelor of arts degree in elementary education, Elsa attended Michigan State University's Graduate School of Education, obtaining two master's degrees in curriculum and teaching and educational leadership. It was there that Elsa's love of curricular work and commitment to growing leaders began. She has also worked as an adjunct professor for Michigan State University, teaching a week-long course in their program in Plymouth, England, and has led professional development for teachers and administrators at the Principals' Training Center (PTC), East Asia Regional Council of Overseas Schools (EARCOS), and Association of International Schools in Africa (AISA).

To learn more about Elsa's work, follow @elsadonohue on Twitter.

Suzette Julien is a dedicated and committed educator who has been in the field of education since 1990. She began her teaching career in the Boston Public Schools system and found her way to the Caribbean, where she implemented remedial reading programs for local private schools. Suzette's international experience began in 1995 at the International School of Port of Spain, where she taught for two years and later became the first woman principal for the elementary school. Suzette has been an advocate for professional teams, and she has coordinated the

Teachers Teaching Teachers (TTT) program because she promotes learning from each other. Suzette has several credentials in education, including special education (Sheffield University, United Kingdom) as well as a master's degree in education (Framingham, Massachusetts) and a doctorate in teaching and learning, curriculum, and leadership (Northeastern University, Boston, Massachusetts). Suzette's dissertation focus explored how women of color leaders make sense of their professional and personal experiences in K–12 international schools.

Michelle Kuhns is an educational consultant and leadership coach working with schools and school leaders around the world. She began her teaching career in Washington state before moving overseas and teaching in Saudi Arabia, Indonesia, Poland, and the United Arab Emirates. She has been an international educator for over twenty years and has led curriculum and professional development in overseas schools for ten years. Michelle has also served as the director of learning at the American School of Dubai. As a curriculum director, she has been deeply involved in school-based curriculum design across all disciplines. Michelle has served as a member of regional curriculum, assessment, and professional development committees such as Educational Collaborative for International Schools (ECIS) and Near East South Asia (NESA) and has taught assessment literacy for educators at the graduate level.

An educator for twenty years, **Kate McKenna** began her career in college admissions, working as an admissions counselor at the University of the South–Sewanee. Seeking opportunities to work more directly with students, she switched sides of the desk and worked in the college counseling offices at two independent schools in the Washington, D.C., area. She then ventured to Rome, Italy, where she met her husband—a fellow English teacher. She has also worked in Paraguay, Bulgaria, China, and Chile. She holds a bachelor of arts in English literature from the University of the South–Sewanee, a master's in English literature from Middlebury College, a certificate in international school counseling from Lehigh University, an educational specialist degree in mental health practices in schools from the University of Missouri, a certificate in international school leadership from the Principals' Training Center, and a doctorate in educational leadership from Nova Southeastern University.

Aleasha Morris is an educational leader and certified executive coach. Her professional career has spanned twenty years and five countries, and she has held numerous teaching, leadership, and counseling roles. She leverages the unique insight she has gained from working in both the public and private international education sectors to support professional development in various fields. From health care to engineering to global business, Aleasha combines her experience in the areas of strengths training and development, leadership, counseling, and organizational strategy to create powerful learning opportunities for all those who want to maximize their performance. Aleasha holds an undergraduate degree in English and French from the University of Saskatchewan, an education degree from McGill University, and a master's degree in educational leadership from Michigan State. In addition, she has completed post-graduate work in counseling from Lehigh University and is a certified Solution Focused Therapist and Executive Coach.

Visit https://floconsulting.ca/about-me/ to learn more about Aleasha Morris's work.

Francesca Mulazzi, EdD, has been an educator since 1999. From her first international position in elementary education in Rabat, Morocco, through teaching French and ESL in Shanghai and Singapore, to K–12 principal in Aruba, and IB Coordinator in Lusaka, Francesca's international school experience is rich and layered. She has specialized in seeing students as individuals and helping to adjust learning to meet their needs through literacy and differentiation. She received her BA in French and Italian literature from the University of Vermont, her MEd in educational leadership and administration from the University of Oregon, and her EdD in learning, leadership, and community from Plymouth State University.

Maya Nelson is currently the deputy head of school at Jakarta Intercultural School (JIS) in Jakarta, Indonesia. She has served in a variety of administrative capacities in different international schools, having first been a teacher for more than twenty years in both international and U.S. public schools, including the American School in Japan, Taipei American School, Denver Public Schools, and Cherry Creek Public Schools in Colorado. In addition to her work as a school administrator, she is also a consultant, auditor, and presenter. She has presented at EARCOS, Women of Influence (WOI) in Education, National Council of Supervisors of Mathematics (NCSM), and many more. Maya grew up as a third-culture kid living in Japan, England, Germany, Indonesia, and the United States. She is a passionate advocate for children, having started various innovative programs overseas, including a school-within-a-school designed to support students with moderate learning differences. Maya has a BA in special education and elementary education from the University of Northern Colorado, an MA in educational leadership from San Diego State University, and a Certificate of Advanced Leadership from Harvard University.

Pauline O'Brien has worked in corporate management, international education leadership recruitment, career guidance, and training design and delivery since 1993. She is a driven leader who loves to share her innovative practice and business growth ideas with others. She has a true aptitude for discovering talent and is passionate about helping other women leaders move up the ladder. Pauline previously worked for the Council of International Schools as director of career recruitment and services. She currently works as director of administrative services and governance services for the International School Systems. She earned her credentials through the Educatief Centrum for Leadership (Praktisch/Middel Management) in the Dutch language. Fluent in English and Dutch, along with having extensive knowledge of French and Spanish, Pauline brings a very strong international perspective to her work.

Foreword

JOELLEN KILLION

In *Raise Her Up: Stories and Lessons From Women in International Educational Leadership*, Debra E. Lane and Kimberly Cullen bring to light the inequity within leadership roles in international education. A persistent challenge that faces schools around the world, this issue must be acknowledged and corrected. The authors approach the problem with both hope and reality. By analyzing the experiences of ten women leaders who serve in diverse corners of the globe, they seek to tell the truth about how complex the path to leadership is for women. They also seek to give hope to other women who strive for recognition and opportunity to serve as leaders.

As a comparative case study, *Raise Her Up* is an artful mixture of personal narratives and thoughtful analysis that depict the trials and joy woven deeply into the lives of ten women, central figures in a much broader cast of women leaders in international education. Lane and Cullen have not only crafted a collection of experiences of women leaders who have devoted their lives to creating opportunity for others and serving the education profession, but they have also extrapolated profound lessons from between the lines of their experiences. Socrates's statement that "the unexamined life is not worth living" has merit, after all (Plato, 399 BCE/1984). When one pauses to examine what one experiences, useful lessons emerge. This book unpacks the purpose, service, and passion that drive the women on their journey to become acknowledged, valued, and celebrated equally as leaders alongside their male counterparts. Each woman, whose story is carefully constructed from her daily experiences, discloses the beauty of the struggle, the grit necessary to persist, the vision and goals held, and the growth that emerges. The authors explain both the patterns and uniqueness within each woman's experiences. The stories of Kate McKenna, Elsa Donohue, Michelle Kuhns, Debra Lane, Kimberly Cullen, Aleasha Morris, Pauline O'Brien, Francesca Mulazzi, Maya Nelson, and Suzette Julien represent a broad spectrum of pathways to leadership, yet their stories possess a commonality—as if they were sisters within the same family.

Raise Her Up clarifies the importance of mentors who seek to find and nurture the potential in others. It recognizes that community and relationships provide the supportive network within which both novice and experienced leaders thrive. It highlights the uncertainty and vulnerability leaders, especially women, face in their work. It identifies the core attributes of women leaders and guides readers to develop them through self-study, self-awareness, reflection, and ongoing learning.

In 2020, the year that Kamala Harris became the vice-president elect in the United States, Sarah Fuller of Vanderbilt University became the first female to play in a Power Five college football game, and president-elect Joseph Biden announced an all-female communications team for his new administration, the promise of equity for women in leadership was strong. But if we are to secure these gains, both women and men must commit to work together to close the gender gap among education leaders. Lane and Cullen offer significant lessons on how to achieve this goal.

When women rise, the world will rise. This statement summarizes the core message in *Raise Her Up: Stories and Lessons From Women in International Educational Leadership.* It emerges from the profound lessons revealed in the pages of this book and within the personal narratives of the dedicated, courageous, and resilient women leaders featured. Gender equity in leadership, when achieved, will benefit every aspect of human existence.

Joellen Killion
Leadership and learning consultant
Senior advisor to Learning Forward

Introduction

DEBRA E. LANE

Each time a woman stands up for herself,
without knowing it possibly, without claiming it,
she stands up for all women.

—MAYA ANGELOU

The World Economic Forum reported in 2019 that at the current pace, it will take another 208 years to achieve gender equality in the United States (Gates, 2019; Zahidi, 2019). The first time my coauthor, Kim, read this, she quipped, "Well, I guess 208 isn't really that long, given how long it's taken to get this far." But Kim has two girls who had both just turned eighteen. That means neither her daughters, her granddaughters, her great-granddaughters, nor her great-great-granddaughters will live in a world where gender equality is the norm. Wait, *what?!*

In the spring of 2019, I attended a leading conference for school heads and administrators. Of the hundreds of attendees, I noted that only about one in five were women. Men organized and ran the conference, they gave the vast majority of the talks, and it seemed men made most of the decisions around education. It was clearly disproportionate. Shouldn't this predominance of men in leading roles in education be a thing of the past? Having interviewed for head of school positions myself, I knew differently. Breaking through the invisible barrier into leadership was going to be a challenge, and not because I lacked qualifications. Even though I had passed various rounds of interviews and been selected as a finalist in a number of searches, men told me time and again that I lacked head of school experience. This was the classic double-edged sword, only with a seemingly gendered twist.

I knew I was not alone. Among the women in attendance, there were heads of schools, aspiring heads of schools, and senior leaders from various educational organizations. The more veteran women attendees insisted that despite decades-old gender disparity, they found some hope in the fact that more women were at this one particular event than ever before. I listened as they exchanged stories about just how hard

1

it is to break into educational leadership as a woman, and it became exceedingly clear that we have to do more to lift women into the leadership roles they are more than qualified to take but rarely receive.

Early on in this project, Kim and I connected through a mutual friend, who found that we shared a passion for helping women break through the glass ceiling that prevents them from becoming the decision makers in education. According to researchers Kerry Robinson, Charol Shakeshaft, Margaret Grogan, and Whitney Sherman Newcomb (2017), the American Association of School Administrators estimates that, in 2015, women comprised approximately a quarter of the total number of superintendents in the United States, whereas they made up approximately 75 percent of the teaching staff. And that ceiling is global. In 2019, the United Nations Educational, Scientific and Cultural Organization (UNESCO) reported that around the world, 94 percent of early childhood teachers and less than 50 percent of secondary teachers are women, yet in high-income countries like Finland, Japan, Portugal, and South Korea, women make up no more than 13 percent of the school leaders (Global Education Monitoring Report, 2019). Worldwide, it is clear that "teaching is frequently a female profession with men in charge" (p. 3). While the research shows that there is progress in the direction of greater equality, Kim and I know that 208 years is just too long—and that progress has slowed in recent years (England, Levine, & Mishel, 2020). Many organizations, like Equality Can't Wait (www.equalitycantwait.com), are doing good work, but we believe it's incumbent on each of us to do more and to do it better. Everyone, regardless of gender (and at every level of every organization), plays a key role in lifting one another up and empowering each other to be our best.

As a field, education works tirelessly to find the best ways to prepare students for the future. It is dynamic and constantly changing, characterized by the eternal question, *How can we do this better?* As an art form, education is reflective and progressive. As a science, it is research-based and evidence-driven. Because it is so complex and continually shifting, education requires constant and fearless leadership, regardless of gender. *Raise Her Up* is a response to the reality that women don't often see a way in. It champions the idea that, as a society, we need to do better—better for our young people, better for our future, better for women. After decades of struggling to break through the male-dominated upper echelons of leadership, it is time for change. Call it a glass ceiling or a steel box—breaking through the boundaries is hard to do. But it is possible, and our future depends on it.

This book shares stories of persistence, mentorship, courage, and advocacy. It is our hope that in reading these stories, educators of all kinds will learn to listen to their own voices as they navigate complex systems that don't always favor equality. This book is written for every leader—independent of gender—who aspires to equitable leadership in international schools. International schools are inherently diverse, and excellent leadership comes in all shapes and sizes, *and* genders.

What Makes International Education Unique?

SIS Hurst Senior Professional Lecturer Fanta Aw describes international education in terms of mobility: students travel the globe to gain knowledge, expose themselves to diverse cultures, meet all kinds of people, and expand their intercultural competence (as cited in Quain, 2018). Companies also have a stake in international education. Mohamed Abdel-Kader (2015), Deputy Assistant Secretary for International and Foreign Language Education at the U.S. Department of Education, estimated in 2015 that one in five U.S. jobs is tied to global trade; that number held steady through 2019, until the pandemic caused what is expected to be a temporary decline (Baughman & Francois, 2020; World Trade Organization, 2021). Some employers encourage employees to go abroad and learn about other cultures and languages; in a global market, having workers with these skills is an important advantage to compete internationally. Therefore, international K–12 schools are an added benefit for employees working abroad.

According to ISC Research (n.d.), in 2021, there are 12,373 international schools around the world educating 5.68 million students. These schools hire 550,846 staff, and the total fee incomes are $53 billion. This industry is growing, particularly in Asia and the Middle East. From 2011 to 2021, there has been a 62 percent increase in international schools, fee incomes have risen 104 percent, and staff have increased by 68 percent. Despite the growth in international schools, White males still dominate the leadership positions.

What Does This Book Aim to Achieve?

Raise Her Up draws on the experiences of women—both their challenges and their successes—as they pursue careers in international school leadership. The book is full of case studies in leadership and explores a variety of topics relevant to international education—from managing crises to developing intercultural competence. You will learn how women are blazing their own trails overseas, not only leading international schools but also working with local politicians, security, support staff, and operations of schools in foreign countries.

Aspiring leaders looking for a starting point will discover accounts of interviewing, working with boards, learning about community culture, taking risks, practicing mindful leadership, and furthering growth as a leader. *Raise Her Up* provides a wealth of practical advice from leaders at the elementary, middle, and high school levels from around the world. And finally, this book challenges women who get past the traditional boundaries by asking themselves the hard questions about who they think they are (and who they think others think they are), who they really want to be, and how they can get there. This book is intended for all female leaders of K–12 schools as well as our male allies, who are growing in numbers.

This book is different from other sources we have found on leadership for women in that it focuses primarily on real women's stories, sharing both their celebrations and challenges. It aims to inspire women (and men) to spark a much-needed clamor for women to assume roles of influence throughout international education systems. It highlights the change that is possible when women unite as a community to help one another as leaders. It draws upon the excellent work and research of international women leaders and highlights the power and importance of proudly and openly celebrating our achievements. It helps readers uncover their unconscious bias and shows how this bias affects women leaders in the areas of science, mathematics, and leadership. It enables educators to discover how building their network creates new opportunities, connections, and personal definitions of success. It calls women to listen to the most powerful and courageous voices—their own.

Our goal is to unleash networks of women leaders who create improved communities that support one another toward leadership positions. These budding leaders are our best hope for crossing the growing chasm of inequity in education.

What Will You Find in This Book?

From start to finish, this book is about lifting up women. The cover art was designed with this goal in mind, by featuring the work of artist Flavia Coll. Flavia has been raising women up through her work for years by devoting a number of pieces to women each year and contributing her art for International Women's Day. In *Raise Her Up*, ten women leaders contribute their stories—interspersed with commentary from Kim and me—recounting their unique pathway to international educational leadership. Each story is followed by leadership lessons from the narrative that merit in-depth examination. You'll explore what current research and expert advice say about the characteristics found in the contributor's story, and you'll reflect on your relationship with the traits highlighted in each lesson. Consider journaling about your reflections to internalize the lessons.

> In chapter 1, Elsa Donohue's story explores the lessons of finding your own path, leaning on others, valuing self-care, and acknowledging vulnerability. This chapter celebrates the invaluable role of mentors in a leader's journey.

> In chapter 2, Michelle Kuhns's story highlights the importance of developing self-awareness, establishing boundaries, and valuing your worth. Michelle's story reminds readers that when women know their needs and set boundaries to honor their limits, they flourish as leaders.

> In chapter 3, Debra Lane's story illustrates the importance of building resilience, honoring your instincts, choosing persistence, and leading with humility. This chapter suggests a surprising truth: that humility is a leadership superpower.

> In chapter 4, Kimberly Cullen's story shows the power of believing in yourself, embracing failure, and having faith in purpose. When women know they are

capable and trust the process, they can push through self-doubt and meet their goals.

> In chapter 5, Aleasha Morris's story imagines how redefining success, taking risks, and thinking outside the box empower women to discover their unique path to leadership.

> In chapter 6, Pauline O'Brien's story champions trailblazers, those leaders who chart a course into the unknown for others to follow. Pauline's story highlights lessons of developing cultural awareness, building relationships, and acting with integrity.

> In chapter 7, Francesca Mulazzi's story illustrates how essential it is for leaders to practice self-care so they can be committed to their work for the long haul. Lessons learned in this chapter include committing to reflection, valuing help from others, finding purpose through hardship, and seeking balance.

> In chapter 8, Maya Nelson's story highlights how being persistent and trusting in right timing can support leaders in challenging times. Readers will consider lessons on the following themes: understanding the importance of relationships, harnessing your vision, cultivating a shared purpose, and trusting in right timing.

> In chapter 9, Suzette Julien's story praises the virtues of heart-centered leadership. When leaders are committed to having integrity, being open-minded, and leading with heart, they create strong and meaningful bonds with colleagues and stakeholders.

> Chapter 10, "Bringing It All Together," highlights five central strands in leadership development for women who aspire to leadership positions in K–12 international education: (1) self-awareness, (2) authenticity, (3) courage, (4) connectedness, and (5) resilience. In this final chapter, you'll look more deeply at each of the five strands and engage with exercises to help you develop each trait as part of your growth as a leader.

After you read this book, you will be able to:

> Have the tools to become a more collaborative, evidence-based, and effective leader

> Understand how to make changes to foster growth in your learning community

> Provide more stakeholders with a voice in your community

> Consider a leadership advisory team of your own and put into your practice leadership styles and methods to use at work

> Empower women to help one another become successful educational leaders

> *Raise her up!*

To close out this introduction and start us off, Kate McKenna shares her story of reckoning with her femaleness in educational leadership and issues a call to action.

KATE'S STORY
KATE MCKENNA

I began my career in international education in 2004. Having held a variety of positions within several U.S. independent and international schools (English teacher, counselor, university admission representative, dorm head, coach, and department and program leader), I was considering my next career steps. A female school administrator and mentor of mine suggested that I should consider a move into school leadership. Her suggestion slowly percolated until I found myself shifting my professional goals and educational experiences to support a potential move into international school administration. More than ten years and a variety of leadership experiences later, I found myself in a position where my ultimate goal of serving as a high school principal was on the brink of being realized.

I had been invited to interview for a principal position at a prestigious international school. I prepared diligently and felt a mixture of excitement and curiosity for the visit. Everyone told me to expect nothing less than a "carwash." When I looked at my densely packed two-day schedule, I realized what they meant: I was about to be inspected by every stakeholder group imaginable, subjected to a flood of questions that would allow them to determine how suited I was to the leadership role in question.

As I walked onto campus for the first time, I took a deep breath and looked around. My potential future colleagues were standing at the front of the school. I joined them, and together, we began chatting while welcoming students to campus for the day. I felt myself ease into the possibility: I was prepared, and I knew that this school was one where I could see myself contributing to the community and helping the school realize its vision.

As the buses pulled up to the drop-off circle, more and more people began to arrive. I was introduced to students, parents, teachers. I shook hand after hand and swore to myself that I would remember the slew of names that were flooding my brain. Suddenly, the assistant principal popped outside the building to say hello. At that moment, I took one look at my prospective partner—let's call her Melissa—and realized that I had a huge hurdle ahead of me. Melissa was female. We had similar builds, similar hair, similar skin, similar clothes, and even a few similar mannerisms. We were different people, of course, and we might have made an awesome team, but at that moment, I had a sinking feeling that even within this supposed modern and international world of education, we didn't look the part.

Interestingly, I had never thought much about my own femaleness until I started stepping into leadership roles in international schools. As a child and then adolescent, I had been raised to believe that I could do anything I put my mind to. I was capable, curious, and collaborative: if I wanted to be a leader, more power (girl power!) to me. Sure, I had studied feminism and read about the suffrage movement, but these were combating constructs of the past. After all, this was the twenty-first century.

Before heading into the building to start my morning round of interviews, I thought back to the advice my new boss and mentor had given me before departing: "Be unabashedly yourself." It was good advice. Leadership is about fit, and this job needed to be a match for me just as much as I needed to be a match for it. I took a deep breath, rooted my feet firmly in my heels, and stepped inside.

I didn't get the job.

But the most unexpected thing happened. After receiving the "unfortunately, we chose someone else" email, the head of the school took the time to connect with me and give me feedback about my visit. Not only did he give me his opinion of the experience, he sent me the unedited feedback he had collected from various constituents in the process. It was at that moment that he offered me this gem of advice: "Find out what the elephants were in the room, and next time you get the chance, speak directly to them."

I dug into the data. Two elephants loomed large in my process. The first one I expected: I was the only assistant principal competing against a candidate pool of sitting principals. Certainly, I anticipated receiving feedback that I needed "more seasoning." The second elephant was the harder one to accept, yet I saw it repeated throughout the feedback forms. It sounded something like: "We already have a Melissa." There it was again, the idea that one female leader in the school was enough. That sentiment was repeated over and over throughout the forms: "She seems great, but we already have a Melissa."

Some of the comments were comparative. Others were curious: "Has it ever been done?" Some comments were offensive: "Can she really raise two little children as a primary caregiving mother without sacrificing her commitment to our HS students?" "She has young kids, and I want to ask her: 'Are you willing for your priority to be our HS kids over your kids? Are you sure about this?'" One comment, in particular, was disheartening: "If she becomes the high school principal, then the principal and vice principal will both be women. Is that okay for the school?" This would be a recurring, soul-testing theme.

Almost as soon as I entered the field of international school administration, in 2011, I began receiving negative feedback about my femaleness wrapped into my professional evaluation. This problem wasn't just rooted at one school; rather, the issue seemed to be global. For example, I once applied for an administrative job at the school where I worked; I walked into the interview about four months pregnant with my first child. Some of the committee members—my current colleagues and friends—had a hard time with that. During the interview, I was asked questions about how I would be able to balance my work with a new child at home. I gave what I assume was a satisfactory response, but I wondered if the committee asked other applicants the same types of questions about their home-life balance.

Years later, my boss and mentor, who had observed that interview, told me that he was surprised that my pregnancy played a role in the selection process. Jokingly, he added, "Your son was the fourth candidate in the room." Unbeknownst to me, the questions about my ability to do the job with a new baby at home had been a sticking point during the committee's deliberation process. My boss admitted that he had to remind the committee that he had interviewed for his administrative position at that same school with his infant son actually attending the interview. He recounted that he had never in his career received questions about his ability to balance or manage his work and family responsibilities. So why was I being held to a different standard?

Several years into that job, I opened my annual professional feedback survey—only to read an anonymous comment from a faculty member blasting me for working too much and not spending enough time with my children. The author, who I assume was one of my colleagues, went on to state: "You are not being as good of a mom as you could be." I wondered if that same person sent comments like that to male administrators on our team. So here I was, years later, pursuing a new leadership opportunity in a new country at a different international school, yet once again, staring at my potential new teammate and feeling self-conscious about being so . . . female.

Fast forward: By 2020, I had attained my goal of becoming a high school principal, and yet I remained hopeful that the international school community would demand more from itself in the future. Data collected from ISC Research (2018) identify over 10,000 international schools on the market as of 2019. Around 73 percent of the leaders of those schools are male. This is unacceptable. More female leaders should be helping to shape the future of international education. I feel fortunate: I had a female administrator tap on my shoulder and push me to consider leadership opportunities. I know I am privileged to have had two bosses truly mentor me—and by mentor, I mean that they worked hard to give me opportunities so that I was performing in my current role but simultaneously given opportunities that allowed me to prepare for my next job.

I am immensely proud to be on a team of school leaders where, in the 2020–2021 school year, all four divisional school leaders—the early years director, elementary school principal, middle school principal, and high school principal—are female. That is something I have imagined but never seen in almost twenty years working in the field of international education.

Yet despite those accomplishments, the statistics tell us that too few women are going to get that tap on the shoulder or the necessary mentoring that they should (Duffin, 2021;

Glass, 2019; Superville, 2016). Consider this a call to action. Women everywhere need you. We need your voice at our table. We need your ideas and approaches to complex problems. We need role models for our students. We need to change the image of international school leadership teams. We need more leaders who are ready to be unabashedly themselves. We need international school leaders who are unabashedly female.

References and Resources

Abdel-Kader, M. (2015, November 19). *The importance of an international education for all students* [Blog post]. Accessed at www.linkedin.com/pulse/importance-international-education-all-students-mohamed-abdel-kader on September 14, 2021.

Baughman, L. M., & Francois, J. F. (2020). *Trade and American jobs: The impact of trade on U.S. and state-level employment: 2020 update.* Accessed at www.wita.org/atp-research/trade-and-american-jobs/ on September 14, 2021.

Duffin, E. (2021, July 23). *Number of principals in public schools in the United States from 1993 to 2018, by gender.* Accessed at www.statista.com/statistics/1120283/number-principals-public-schools-gender-us/ on September 14, 2021.

England, P., Levine, A., & Mishel, E. (2020). Progress toward gender equality in the United States has slowed or stalled. *Proceedings of the National Academies of Sciences, 117*(13), 6990–6997.

Gates, M. (2019, June 21). Let's not take 208 years to achieve equality for women in America. *USA Today.* Accessed at www.usatoday.com/story/opinion/2019/06/21/equality-for-women-cant-wait-208-years-melinda-gates-column/1511613001/ on September 13, 2021.

Glass, T. E. (2019). *Where are all the women superintendents?* Accessed at www.aasa.org/SchoolAdministratorArticle.aspx?id=14492 on July 19, 2021.

Global Education Monitoring Report. (2019). *Gender report: Building bridges for gender equality.* Accessed at https://unesdoc.unesco.org/ark:/48223/pf0000368753/PDF/368753eng.pdf.multi on July 19, 2021.

ISC Research. (n.d.). *International school data you can trust.* Accessed at https://iscresearch.com/ on November 23, 2021.

ISC Research. (2018). *The Global Report for Schools 2018.* London: Author.

Lo, D. (2015, November 9). *The best advice ever from Madeleine Albright, Iman, Billie Jean King, and Serena Williams* at Glamour's *Women of the Year Awards.* Accessed at www.glamour.com/story/best-advice-women-ever on October 25, 2021.

Plato. (1984). Apology of Socrates. In T. G. West and G. S. West (Eds./Trans.), *Four texts on Socrates: Plato's "Euthyphro," "Apology of Socrates," "Crito," and Aristophanes' "Clouds."* Ithaca, NY: Cornell University Press. (Original work published ca. 399 BCE)

Quain, S. (2018, March 9). *What's the importance of international education?* Accessed at www.american.edu/sis/news/20180306-whats-the-importance-of-international -education.cfm on February 14, 2022.

Robinson, K., Shakeshaft, C., Grogan, M., & Newcomb, W. S. (2017). Necessary but not sufficient: The continuing inequality between men and women in educational leadership—Findings from the American Association of School Administrators mid-decade survey. *Frontiers in Education, 2.* Accessed at doi:10.3389/feduc .2017.00012 on July 19, 2021.

Rogers, B. K. (2020). When women don't speak. *BYU Magazine.* Accessed at https:// magazine.byu.edu/article/when-women-dont-speak/ on July 19, 2021.

Superville, D. R. (2016, November 15). Few women run the nation's school districts. Why? *Education Week.* Accessed at www.edweek.org/leadership/few-women-run -the-nations-school-districts-why/2016/11 on September 14, 2021.

The World Bank. (2021, June 8). *The global economy: On track for strong but uneven growth as COVID-19 still weighs.* Accessed at www.worldbank.org/en/news/feature /2021/06/08/the-global-economy-on-track-for-strong-but-uneven-growth-as -covid-19-still-weighs on September 14, 2021.

World Trade Organization. (2021, March 31). *World trade primed for strong but uneven recovery after COVID-19 pandemic shock* [Press release]. Accessed at https://www .wto.org/english/news_e/pres21_e/pr876_e.htm on February 14, 2022.

Zahidi, S. (2019, June 18). *Accelerating gender parity in Globalization 4.0* [Blog post]. Accessed at www.weforum.org/agenda/2019/06/accelerating-gender-gap-parity -equality-globalization-4/ on September 13, 2021.

CHAPTER 1

On Staying Committed and Being Empowered

If you educate a woman, you educate a family;
if you educate a girl, you educate the future.

—QUEEN RANIA OF JORDAN

ELSA'S STORY
ELSA DONOHUE

I was the eighth of nine children in a large, traditional Venezuelan family guided by strong Catholic values and directed by a father who ran the family as if we were in the military. Add to a strict and regimented upbringing the fact that I was a year younger than my peer group, the result of having skipped grade 2. So, in high school, my friends were driving, going out, and dating—activities that were out of the question for me because I was too young. In this context, there was little room for a young girl like me to have my own voice or my own ideas. Little Elsa, though, was spunky, zesty, and full of life. Through my actions, I let those around me know that I did have a mind of my own.

I was a decent student who loved physics, a love that was inspired by my major cognitive crush on our teacher, Profesor Frontado, a heavy-set man in his sixties who was intelligent and highly regarded and had once been honored as a National Science Teacher of the Year. I did well in school, particularly in science. I was also, however, the giggly student who chatted when lessons were going on, who had to stand at the front of the row balancing everyone's books on my head, and who got suspended in grade 10 for smoking a cigarette in the back of the school, two floors directly below the Mother Superior's window. If only we had chosen a better spot!

Elsa spent her childhood finding ways to exert her independence, acting out against the boundaries established by her parents and a strict religious upbringing, so it felt ironic that her parents would decide to send her all the way to the United States for college. Her childhood seemed to end abruptly as she found herself at the University of Florida. Speaking limited English, Elsa enrolled in the University of Florida English Language Institute, a program for English learners.

That entire year, I attended courses to learn a language I actually was not interested in learning. I had few friends, and I was alone in a country in which I did not yet feel comfortable. Lacking fluency in English and being a stranger in someone else's land made me very self-conscious. I had gone from being a chatty student to being very quiet; from having an opinion about pretty much anything, to now pushing those opinions to the recesses of my mind. I was so self-conscious about my accent that I barely participated in class discussions. Finally, I was afraid of making mistakes, something I had never experienced as a younger person but that had now become a pronounced trait in me.

One day, I was walking past the Early Years Center at the university and stopped to watch the children playing outside. It reminded me of my childhood, running around in a yard with over forty mango trees and my big family, cousins, and others, who would congregate at my house for special occasions. A sign advertising jobs for interns caught my attention. Seeing that advertisement on that door opened a future I had never anticipated. A semester later, I decided to become a teacher.

My first international teaching job found me in a school with a very supportive principal who saw something special in me. He was instrumental in supporting my growth and in building my confidence as a young practitioner. I remember clearly one day, while I was in the teacher's lounge enjoying a cigarette (those were the days when schools still had smoking lounges), the principal suggested that I join a committee that was to begin looking at math programs. I was so flattered that my principal thought I had something to offer. I remember feeling like I had nothing to offer: very little experience, not a native speaker of English, and only a few months in that school, which was replete with "veterans." That was the first of many times I was mentored by an able and supportive supervisor, often a man, who would identify in me a skill, trait, or value that made me shine as an educator and, later, as a leader.

One horrible morning in Jakarta, Indonesia, the mother of all crises descended upon the Jakarta Intercultural School. At the end of my third year as one of the elementary principals, the most horrific false allegations were lodged against outsourced cleaners at the school. And then, against three of our staff: a learning leader, a teaching assistant, and myself. As of 2021, our teaching assistant was still detained. Had it not been for those around me highlighting my inner strength, helping me find my resilient core, and modeling how to be a gracious and strong leader, I would not be where I am now.

During the entire summer break of this particular year, the three of us were waiting to serve as "witnesses" in the legal case that now defined our lives. Waiting around to be summoned by the police made for a terrifying couple of months. Our passports had been confiscated, so we could go nowhere. In the middle of the summer holiday, the wait ended for my two colleagues. They endured a whole day of interrogation and were told later that night that they would be held at the police station to face questioning early in the morning. Thus began, for them, a very long period of undeserved imprisonment.

I was waiting my turn and quietly worrying about what would happen and wondering when I would be summoned. It was almost a year later that I learned I had been spared the interrogation and imprisonment for two reasons: (1) the summons had been lost, and (2) I had the full weight and support of the U.S. Embassy.

As the summer ended and we welcomed new teachers, I doubted I could continue to be the leader of the elementary school. I thought, "How can I face our new colleagues, as well as our returning teachers, students, and families, knowing that the others are still detained, and I am not?" At some stage, the head of school and deputy head told me that the others would continue to be detained and that the case was turning into more of a marathon than a sprint. Hearing this made me cry uncontrollably. In between sobs, I said, "How am I going to do this? How can I start school with them in jail and me being free?" The head of school replied, "You have to. You have to, and you have what it takes to do it."

The American Psychological Association (2012) defines *resilience* as the ability to adapt in the face of traumatic, tragic, or stressful situations. With resilience comes courage, and amid the terrible guilt she felt, Elsa had to find the courage to continue to do her job—and she did. The experience, as awful as it was, helped her find an inner strength she didn't know she had. Through this experience, Elsa had to rely on herself and her courage to carry her through this crisis.

That perfect storm of a crisis enriched my leadership repertoire. I recognized that leadership is about people, specifically about being there for people. The human factor in our organization took a central role in all I did. I would like to think that during those three years, teachers who were directly impacted by the crisis knew that I genuinely cared about them. "The crisis," as we quickly began referring to the nightmare we faced, led me to grow tremendously.

Professionally, I was thrown into domains of senior leadership in which I had very little experience. I was given instructions by a public relations firm on how to stay on message, how to present myself as being comfortable while being interviewed by the media, how to remain calm in the face of difficult questions that were riddled with assumptions and untruths. In the personal domain, I learned that leaders must take care of themselves before they can effectively take care of others. And so, in spite of how often I failed to do what was necessary for my well-being, attempting to do the right thing helped me overcome the emotional challenge I was living through.

Reflecting on that time period, I recognize there was so much pain, so much fear, so much uncertainty. Through it all, I was surrounded by beautiful examples of female leadership. Though none of these represented formal leadership roles, each was a leader in how to live a life of uncertainty with grace, aplomb, and hope. I could have folded. I could have broken into pieces. But the lessons I learned from these women, combined with the resilience I was cultivating, empowered me to become a better person and a much better leader. It was impossible for me to ignore the strength that surrounded me. So many stood by my side, shining the light on female strength in the face of pain, struggle, and injustice.

With strong mentors by her side, Elsa was able to look inward and find the strength and resilience she needed to move forward during that traumatic time. In *The Seven Habits of Highly Effective People*, Stephen Covey (2020) writes that "between stimulus and response is our greatest power—the freedom to choose" (p. 76). For Covey, this is the foundation of being a powerful person. The first habit he highlights is: being proactive. This habit is about taking responsibility for one's own life. Proactive people don't blame parents, circumstances, or conditions for their behavior. Instead, they choose to focus on areas of life that lie within their circle of influence.

Elsa's story highlights profound lessons about commitment and empowerment. Elsa was equally committed to doing her work with integrity and leading her team with grace. As a result, she was surrounded by the kindness and support of others; their support empowered her to keep going, even amidst a horrific crisis. In this chapter, we'll explore how she found her own path, allowed herself to lean on others, valued self-care, and acknowledged vulnerability. You'll have a chance to reflect on how these lessons inform your experiences as a leader.

Leadership Lessons

In *The Leader in Me*, authors Stephen Covey, Sean Covey, Muriel Summers, and David Hatch (2014) write about seven habits of effective leaders. One that stands out as particularly relevant to Elsa's experience is Habit 7: Sharpen the Saw, which challenges leaders to seek continuous improvement and renewal. Like Elsa, educational leaders face a host of challenges and crises that, if not managed wisely, can send them spiraling toward burnout.

This was particularly evident in 2020–2021 when school leaders dealt with a myriad of unexpected changes due to the COVID-19 global pandemic. In addition, ongoing racial and social injustice, divisive elections around the world, and severe weather events left many leaders feeling end-of-year exhaustion only a few months into the 2021 school year. Under these circumstances, they faced relentless pressure and limited options for relieving that pressure. These leaders and their staff were at risk of burnout. To prevent and overcome burnout, leaders must care for themselves through physical, social, emotional, mental, and spiritual renewal. Habit 7 is revitalizing and helps establish a greater capacity for self-improvement.

Elsa developed this habit repeatedly throughout her life, and it became particularly important as she faced the greatest professional and personal challenge of her life. The crisis that Elsa faced as a school leader in Jakarta is one that all administrators fear but few encounter. The experience was transformational for her: Elsa had to find her way back to herself, the resilient risk-taker who embraced challenges with fortitude. Let's take a closer look at the lessons Elsa learned along the way and how you can use those lessons to sharpen your own saw.

Finding Her Own Path

Growing up in an environment that was strictly regimented by her religion and family culture, Elsa frequently pushed against the boundaries established for her, finding creative ways to make herself heard. Her move to Florida at age sixteen had challenged her confidence and sowed seeds of self-doubt. And yet, the experience opened opportunities for her that she had never imagined. Learning a new language and culture, discovering teaching, and adapting to a new community became integral to her personal growth. Through it all, Elsa had a knack for listening to her heart, a trait that allowed her to follow her own path despite her circumstances.

The ability to listen to one's heart while acting according to reason is a unique trait, but it's a necessary one for leaders to develop. In *Mindful School Communities*, authors Christine Mason, Michele M. Rivers Murphy, and Yvette Jackson (2020) advocate for what they call the *heart-mind connection*, drawing from the expertise of Joseph Mikels, director of the Emotion and Cognition Lab at DePaul University:

> *Philosophers, researchers, therapists, and others have described the importance of adding heart to our decisions. . . . Mikels and his colleagues (2011) asked research participants to make a decision and, when doing so, to focus on their feelings versus details about presented options. They found that adding a feelings' component to certain sorts of complex decisions results in higher-quality decisions and that*

participants sometimes made worse decisions when they deliberated on the details, rather than trusting their instincts or considering their feelings. . . . When teachers [and leaders] are able to balance the strength of their head with heart, new pathways for learning evolve. (pp. 28–29)

Leaders face unique challenges and pressures, a reality that is heightened for women leaders. When women leaders aren't grounded in their strengths and connected to their hearts, they are susceptible to following the paths laid out for them by others. Take a moment to remember Elsa's commitment to her authentic self and notice the benefits she accessed as a result.

REFLECTION QUESTIONS

Reflect on the following questions.

- When have you experienced the need to move in a different direction, to swim upstream, to go against the grain?

- How were you rewarded for your courage to find your own path?

- In what ways do you feel pressured to follow paths set out for you by others?

Educational leaders are faced with difficult decisions throughout their career. They're often expected to follow one path, yet their inner knowing points them in a different direction. It is as though they have two voices (sometimes more!) inside: one tells them to do the thing they are expected to do—the "should do" voice. The "should do" voice is the one that tells you that if you don't do what is expected, then you are doing the wrong thing. The other voice—often a little more subdued—is your own voice, telling you to follow the path you want for yourself. These two voices don't always work together and can sometimes create inner conflict.

The challenge for women leaders is to dial down the "should dos" and raise the volume on their own voice. Learning to listen to your own voice is empowering and rewarding, but it can be hard to do. Figure 1.1 gives you the chance to change the narrative. In the first column, identify the "should dos" that serve as barriers to you speaking or acting. In the second column, consider how you might change "should" to "could." In the third column, write about implications of following your inner voice. The first row includes an example.

"Should Do" Message	"Could Do" Message	Implications of the "Could Do" Message
Sample: It's 9 p.m., I should check my email before I go to bed.	**Sample:** It's 9 p.m. I could check my emails now, or I could go to bed and get up a few minutes early and check them in the morning.	**Sample:** I might sleep better if I don't check my email right now. In both options, I still have the information I need to know before I get to work tomorrow.

FIGURE 1.1: Worksheet for listening to your own voice.

Visit go.SolutionTree.com/leadership for a free reproducible version of this figure.

Leaning on Others

A powerful theme in Elsa's story is how leaning on mentors allows women to grow in ways they can't in isolation. There is no shortage of research on the benefits of mentoring for women in the workplace (Dennehy & Dasgupta, 2017; Ginther, Currie, Blau, & Croson, 2020; Rockwell, Leck, & Elliott, 2013). It is a key strategy women rely on to advance their careers, especially in fields such as engineering, medicine, cybersecurity, data science, law enforcement, and computer science. Women who are mentored receive more benefits in their career with potential for promotions, better compensation, work-life balance, and more.

Kailynn Bowling (2018), cofounder of ChicExecs PR & Retail Strategy Firm, writes that not only can mentors reflect back for women the possibilities of what could be, but they also serve as role models, teachers, coaches, advocates, and sponsors. This was certainly clear in Elsa's story. The mentors in her life saw potential in her that she was not able to see in herself. Having taken a few hard knocks along the way, Elsa was blind to her own strengths. But as she trusted the guidance of her mentors, new doors opened to her, providing opportunities for growth into leadership.

Sometimes, facing the greatest of challenges can feel overwhelming because of a sense of isolation, especially in leadership. So much of Elsa's success rested with her ability to lean into mentorship, and to surround herself with people who inspired her to be greater.

REFLECTION QUESTIONS

Reflect on the following questions.

- Who has served as a role model for you?
- When have you found yourself growing from the strength of others?
- In mentorship relationships, what does each of you give the other in order to create a whole that is greater than the sum of its parts?

Valuing Self-Care

According to the World Health Organization (n.d.), self-care is defined as "the ability of individuals, families, and communities to promote health, prevent disease, maintain health, and to cope with illness and disability with or without the support of a healthcare provider." Proper self-care is prudent for every person's well-being, but it's especially important for ensuring a leader's ability to thrive. Developing a daily exercise routine, checking in on your staff, eating in a healthy way, practicing meditation, and getting professional help when you recognize you need it are just some of the ways you can help yourself and others. Leaders have the opportunity to model healthy boundaries between their work life and personal life.

Elsa realized that to take care of her staff and continue to provide leadership, direction, and a sense of calm, she would first have to take care of herself. If she failed to prioritize her well-being, she would lack the conviction to move forward with confidence. More than any other time in her life, "the crisis" required Elsa to be a trustworthy leader, which meant she had to look after herself. She admits that she did not always do it to the best of her ability, but she knew self-care was going to be the key to getting through the challenge.

Collaboration was an important part of Elsa's self-care strategy. In Habit 6: Synergize, Covey and colleagues (2014) describe *synergy* as creative cooperation. In a synergistic environment, parties value diverse paradigms and the opinions of others. Elsa took the opinions of others and willingly listened to differences and similarities to open her mind. She had a gift to synergize her staff by staying open herself.

REFLECTION QUESTIONS

Reflect on the following questions.

○ When have you needed the energy of a group to be able to lead? How did it affect your leadership?

○ Elsa was humbled by leadership qualities that emerged from some of the most unexpected people. Make a list of people who irritate you. How might they represent different views that could lead to synergy?

○ Who are the people in your tribe and why?

Acknowledging Vulnerability

During the darkest days of "the crisis," Elsa came to a point of such deep self-doubt that she questioned her ability to lead her school. It wasn't self-reliance or grit that pulled her through; it was vulnerability. When she confessed her doubts to her head of school, she was heard, understood, and encouraged. It is all too common for women leaders to struggle beneath the weight of self-doubt, a burden only made heavier by trying to hide their vulnerability. When they learn to embrace it as a strength, though, they can share the load instead of carrying it alone, and they create a culture that invites others to do the same.

Authors Jane Danvers, Heather De Blasio, and Gavin Grift (2021) champion vulnerability in *Five Ways of Being: What Learning Leaders Think, Do, and Say Every Day*.

[Uncomfortable situations] demand that we expose our vulnerability to both our-selves and our colleagues. . . . We need leaders who open themselves up to taking risks, to going beyond, and to challenging themselves. This is the real, deep self-work that is the challenge of our times in schools. . . . There is something about the explicit nature of leading learning that requires us to be vulnerable and steadfast in our commitment to embracing, modeling, expecting, and implementing the very change we want to see. (p. 18)

Acknowledging her vulnerability showed Elsa an unlikely path through the crisis. She identified a community of mentors and women who opened an avenue for her to emerge feeling strong and supported. She accepted that she had to lead the way, but that she would not be able to do it alone, and so she found a tribe that allowed her to be what she needed at the time: real, vulnerable, raw. She emerged with renewed strength and resilience.

REFLECTION QUESTIONS

Reflect on the following questions.

- When have you felt empowerment in accepting vulnerability?
- When have you gained strength through recognizing your own humanity?
- How did you use this situation to grow, to be empowered?

Food for Thought

In "4 Ways to Attract and Retain Top Female Talent in Tech," Shari Buck (2018), cofounder of the tech company Doximity, recommends tech companies recruit and retain women longer. While she tailored the following four suggestions to the tech world, they are relevant for educational leaders too.

1. **Provide mentors:** Mentors support new hires during onboarding, provide advice, and empower women to acquire the skills they need to create the career path they envision for themselves.

2. **Listen to women's voices:** It's incredibly common and disheartening for women in the workplace to feel their ideas aren't heard or acknowledged. Managers have an opportunity and responsibility to ensure an environment where women's voices have equal impact.

3. **Invest in your employees:** Retaining your top talent is key, but it doesn't happen by accident. When you invest in your employees by providing

development opportunities, ensuring a positive and inclusive culture, and boosting morale, valuable employees are more likely to stay loyal.

4. **Prioritize work-life balance:** There's no question: women have valuable commitments outside of the workplace, and they want their employers to care about that. Strive to create an environment that doesn't merely tolerate women taking time off for their children or extended family members but encourages them to do so.

Women bring extraordinary skills, traits, and vision to their roles in the workplace, but they often face barriers to flourishing when they inhabit male-dominated spaces that don't value their contributions. How might your workplace benefit from embracing Buck's (2018) suggestions? What would it take to ensure that women are not only enabled but actually empowered to ascend to leadership positions in your organization?

Conclusion

Two themes come out clearly in Elsa's story: empowerment and mentorship. The two are closely connected. Empowerment doesn't come from a single place, a specific source. Empowerment comes from one's ability to pull strength from challenge, to recognize one's inner gifts in the face of crisis. For many women in leadership, who are conditioned to question themselves in the face of struggle, it sometimes takes a gentle nudge from a mentor or guide to help them realize they have what it takes to effectively solve problems. From what we've seen, people don't just happen upon senior executive positions—instead, they are nurtured, sponsored, and empowered to enter those roles. It's a process that can take years, and it requires buy-in from the uppermost leaders within an organization.

When men in leadership positions fail to see this, when they neglect to offer support to women ascending the ranks, they perpetuate a culture that closes doors for women (Minor, 2020). Men at all levels of the business community need to become better educated about this pervasive problem and its potential solutions in order to provide support and investment. Additionally, women need more formal and structured sponsorship programs to guide them into roles at the top of their organizations. These are the kinds of steps that will empower women to reach their full potential as leaders.

ELSA'S LEADERSHIP LESSONS

Finding her own path

Leaning on others

Valuing self-care

Acknowledging vulnerability

References and Resources

American Psychological Association. (2012). *Building your resilience.* Accessed at www .apa.org/topics/resilience on July 1, 2021.

Bowling, K. (2018, August 3). Why female mentorship in the workplace is more important than ever. *Forbes.* Accessed at www.forbes.com/sites/yec/2018/08/03/why-female -mentorship-in-the-workplace-is-more-important-than-ever/?sh=16a50db47291 on July 1, 2021.

Buck, S. (2018, October 4). 4 ways to attract and retain top female talent in tech. *Women Entrepreneur.* Accessed at www.entrepreneur.com/article/319697 on July 1, 2021.

Covey, S. (2020). *The seven habits of highly effective people: 30th anniversary edition* (4th ed.). New York: Simon & Schuster.

Covey, S. R., Covey, S., Summers, M., & Hatch, D. K. (2014). *The leader in me: How schools around the world are inspiring greatness, one child at a time* (2nd ed.). New York: Simon & Schuster.

Danvers, J., De Blasio, H., & Grift, G. (2021). *Five ways of being: What learning leaders think, do, and say every day.* Bloomington, IN: Solution Tree Press.

Dennehy, T. C., & Dasgupta, N. (2017). Female peer mentors early in college increase women's positive academic experiences and retention in engineering. *PNAS, 114*(23), 5964–5969.

Ginther, D. K., Currie, J., Blau, F. D., & Croson, R. (2020). Can mentoring help female assistant professors in economics? An evaluation by randomized trial. *National Bureau of Economic Research.* Accessed at www.nber.org/papers/w26864 on February 11, 2022.

Harris, A., & Jones, M. (2020). COVID-19—school leadership in disruptive times. *School Leadership & Management, 40*(4), 243–247.

Leithwood, K., Harris, A., & Hopkins, D. (2020). Seven strong claims about successful school leadership revisited. *School Leadership & Management, 40*(1), 5–22.

Mason, C., Murphy, M. M. R., & Jackson, Y. (2020). *Mindful school communities: The five Cs of nurturing heart centered learning.* Bloomington, IN: Solution Tree Press.

Mikels, J. A., Maglio, S. J., Reed, A. E., & Kaplowitz, L. J. (2011). Should I go with my gut? Investigating the benefits of emotion-focused decision making. *Emotion, 11*(4), 743–753.

Minor, M. (2020, December 5). Women in the workplace: Why they don't get recognized as much as men. *Forbes.* Accessed at www.forbes.com/sites/mariaminor/2020/12/05 /women-in-the-workplace-why-they-dont-get-recognized-as-much-as-men/?sh =3bc5d33657df on October 21, 2021.

Rockwell, B. V., Leck, J. D., & Elliott, C. J. (2013). Can e-mentoring take the "gender" out of mentoring? *Cyberpsychology*, *7*(2).

Wilson, J. M. (2018). *The human side of changing education: How to lead change with clarity, conviction, and courage*. Thousand Oaks, CA: Corwin Press.

World Health Organization. (n.d.). *What do we mean by self-care?* Accessed at www .who.int/reproductivehealth/self-care-interventions/definitions/en/ on November 24, 2021.

CHAPTER 2

On Embracing Control and Knowing Your Worth

*Far too many women are hesitant,
and remain trapped in jobs for which they are
over-qualified or paid beneath their worth.*

—JANET STREET-PORTER

MICHELLE'S STORY
MICHELLE KUHNS

I took my very first teaching job in 1989 in a really small district in Washington State. I was the only German teacher, so I taught every level of German. I had a full schedule, teaching five levels of German in four different periods, and my fifth class was a communications course without a curriculum. It had been taught by five different teachers in five different years and was one of those "make it up as you go" classes, so I made it into a drama class. That seemed to be what the students wanted to do, and there wasn't a drama class at that time at the school. The first year of teaching is hard anyway, but to have six different preps for five periods seemed especially challenging. Realistically, for a new teacher, even two preps would have been challenging.

To add to the layers, though, my school was also involved in an exchange program—the German American Partnership Program—with a school in Germany. The exchange took place each year, alternating so that one year we would go to them, and the next they would come to us. What I didn't know when I took the job as the German teacher was that organizing the exchange fully fell to me. The trip would take place at the end of the school year, during the summer, so in addition to working hard to be a first-year teacher, I also spent long hours planning for this trip. This was before the internet existed, so I was doing old-school planning—hosting meetings at the school and using my own phone to organize hotels, trains, planes, homestays, and excursions. There was no budget for this, so by taking this on, I unknowingly committed to spending money out of pocket to organize the trip. Additionally, it was an expectation of my job that I lead the school trip and represent the school in this long-time partnership at my own expense and during summer break. Though none of this felt right to me, as a first-year teacher fresh out of college, I borrowed money from my parents to pay for the trip that I was required to go on. My husband (we had just gotten married that year) joined me along with the other few chaperones, and we all had to pay out of pocket.

To be fair, it was a good trip. It went well, and we enjoyed ourselves, but we were in debt as a result of it. In late July, after we returned from the trip, my principal reached out to let me know that the school was going to add a course, and he wanted me to teach it. The course was a college-level course in cooperation with the University of Washington that we would offer to high school students, replacing the communications class I had taught the previous year. While one part of me was honored that he thought highly enough of me to offer me the college-level course, I just couldn't fathom not only maintaining the same course load as the previous year but having to learn still another new curriculum in the process. While the principal claimed this course would be a good opportunity for the students, I later realized that his son was entering his senior year of high school and would benefit from the course. There was urgency in the principal's request, and he seemed determined to make it happen. I just didn't know if I wanted to take this on. To add to my frustration, I had also recently learned from other teachers that many of their schools had exchange programs that the school financially supported. Knowing I had been taken advantage of as a new teacher who was eager to do it all, I walked into the conversation about this new course with a different perspective. Instead of answering on the spot, I told my principal I would think about it, and we agreed to talk a week later.

After spending a week going through all the scenarios in my head, I went back to the principal, convinced that teaching the course was not the right move for me. Given how hard my first year had been, I didn't feel confident that I would be able to deliver the kind of teaching and learning that I thought needed to happen in my German classes, much less a new college-level course. Had it been a little later in my career, I might have taken it. But at that point, I knew I needed to make some hard choices. Armed with a letter of resignation, just in case, I walked into his office and explained that I didn't think we had enough time to develop the course well in the month that remained before school started. There were too many requirements in the course to develop so quickly. I told him we could look at developing the course over the next year and implement it the following year.

It was terrifying for me to tell him that I wouldn't take this on. But knowing I was willing to walk if he did not accept it gave me the confidence to be honest and direct.

I had hoped to talk it through with him, to be given the opportunity to work with him to develop the curriculum in a way that would be a win for everyone. But he was unwilling to discuss a collaborative way to move forward. I told him that if that was his final decision, he would have to find someone else to teach the new course. His response to me was, "You know, it's not going to be better in any other school." I said, "Well, if it's not going to be better, then I'm in the wrong profession."

Michelle recognized that she had reached a tipping point. The first year of any profession is daunting, but new teachers have so much to learn in those early months in the classroom. Michelle was teaching five different levels of German and a communications class without any kind of structured curriculum. As a new teacher, Michelle felt isolated, overworked, and unsupported—all factors that contribute to teacher burnout (Jacobson, 2016). That turn of events completely threw her, since, having been raised in a family of teachers, she knew that teachers didn't always have such an unmanageable course load.

I didn't know what I was going to do. A few weeks later, my mom called and told me about an opening for a German teacher at the high school I graduated from. Still unsure whether I actually wanted to be a teacher, I applied for the job. It was my former high school principal who interviewed me. At some point in the conversation, he asked me why I had left the other school. With total honesty, I told him about my year, the preps, the trip, the unreasonable expectations. I left nothing out. He listened thoughtfully, and in spite of all of it—or maybe because of it—he offered me the job. This man knew me. He knew the kind of super busy, active teenager I had been, and he knew that I had a tendency to take on whatever came my way, so when he hired me, he said, "My expectation is for you to be a teacher, and we're going to support your teaching this year. And really, I want you to not do anything else. This year, just teach, and then we'll see what kind of clubs and activities you take on, because I know your heart's there, too. But this year, let's just teach." He's the reason I'm still an educator.

I spent my second year as a teacher learning how to teach. My principal was true to his word; I later found out that, in his commitment to having me just teach, he told the athletic director not to approach me about coaching midway through the year. Not only did I have the support of my principal, but I also worked closely with the other German teacher, who had been my German teacher in school. I taught both English and German, and I had a great year learning how to be a teacher.

Michelle had the good fortune to be supported by a leader who recognized her potential to be a great teacher. But, in a way, she needed a do-over of her first year of teaching. By stripping back the additional duties that teachers frequently take on, the principal allowed Michelle to focus on her craft and learn what it meant to be a teacher. Additionally, she had the support of a mentor, her former German teacher, who served as a partner and sounding board. Had Michelle not taken that first brave step of resigning from her previous school, her experience would have been very different.

Flash forward to 2004, and I had completed my first year teaching German at the American School of Warsaw. In a regular check-in with my head of school, I told him that there seemed to be a lack of curricular documentation and alignment conversations to help guide expectations for teaching and learning. Around the same time, I was invited to be one of the two internal coordinators who led the reaccreditation process at the school. Our work only highlighted the curricular gaps. Thus began a year-long conversation with my head of school about the school's need for a curriculum director.

At the time, the head of school said to me, "You know, that's probably a position that we need to put in place." He and I had had so many conversations about the need for stronger curriculum leadership, and he asked me if it was something I would be interested in applying for. I told him that I absolutely would. I had a master's in curriculum and instruction, and I was working on my administrative license. The position was published the following fall. Despite the importance of the position, and to my complete surprise, it was being offered with a teacher's salary and a 10 percent stipend. If I applied for the position, I would be making less money: I was the student council advisor and a coach, among other things. As the internal coordinator who had just spent a year doing curricular work, I was already making that same stipend. So it was glaringly obvious to me that something was not right. On top of this, having had the conversations with him myself, I knew that he knew that this was going to be a big job.

In every conversation, it was assumed that I would apply for the job. But when the time came, I couldn't do it for the advertised salary. I loved my teaching job and didn't necessarily want to give it up, even knowing that I would learn a lot as a curriculum director and that I would do the job well. But, having been in a similar situation during my first year of teaching, I was not going to allow myself to once again be overworked without appropriate compensation. There was a part of me that wondered whether we would even be having this contract conversation if I were a man. Of course, I'll never know, but I wondered whether there might be a correlation between the lower salary offered and the assumption I would apply for the position. I wasn't looking for power, and I wasn't looking for a ton of money, but I was looking for some equity and some recognition for what the position actually involved. The head of school, surprised at my reaction, continued to recruit for the position. In the end, he couldn't find anyone with the necessary experience and understanding that I had developed. So while he was recruiting in Boston, he called me and asked what I thought the salary should be. And so began the process of negotiation.

In retrospect, I know that I should have negotiated more. But the salary was raised, and I took the position and learned a lot doing the job. This head of school had seen my leadership potential early on and was very supportive of putting me in positions that helped me to grow. The pay piece was a shocker to me that we found our way through, and he has continued to support me as I've moved to different schools and into different leadership roles.

In this chapter, we'll look closely at the lessons Michelle learned as she evolved as a leader. It was through developing self-awareness, establishing boundaries, and valuing her worth that she overcame the early challenges in her career. Michelle had the advantage of coming from a family of educators, and this informed her understanding of what was right and just. At the same time, she had a strong sense of her own strengths and what she was worth. This enabled her to clearly delineate what she would and would not accept as she established herself professionally.

As you read the lessons and questions in the following paragraphs, reflect on how these qualities inform your experiences as a leader.

Leadership Lessons

Having been a curriculum director for a couple of years, through a number of teaching and learning initiatives, Michelle carried tremendous responsibility in her work, and her colleagues considered her to be at the same level as the other administrators in the school. She was a member of the senior administrative leadership team, yet despite the pay increase she initially negotiated, she was the only one who wasn't receiving an administrator's pay and benefits. She knew that it was time to negotiate, and while she didn't like advocating for herself in this way because it felt like she was "grubbing for money," she knew that she deserved to be compensated as an equal. Eventually, she was, but the journey to equity at the table took a full two years of calm, persistent, focused conversations. Let's examine the lessons Michelle learned along the way and how they inform your career perspective: developing self-awareness, establishing boundaries, and valuing her worth.

Developing Self-Awareness

In her first year of teaching, even though Michelle hadn't been in a school before and wasn't entirely sure how things were supposed to work, she knew in her gut that she was being asked to take on too much. Michelle learned that others in similar situations had the support of their schools, and this boosted her confidence to ask for change. It did not take long for Michelle to learn to trust in her decisions, recognize her capacity, and make informed choices about how she would use her time and energy. At a young age, Michelle figured out what she was and was not willing to do. Knowing yourself and what you need to be happy, to grow, and to feel confident is hard to do, but it's essential for you to thrive in your professional life.

If educational leaders are to create a positive environment for their colleagues, teachers, and students, they must practice self-awareness. Danvers, De Blasio, and Grift (2021) call academic leaders to become what they term *learning leaders*, those who, through self-knowledge, ensure that their colleagues, students, and campus are "becoming a truly learning-focused organization" (p. 3). They assert that embracing self-awareness creates a fundamental shift in a leader's way of being as well as a departure from traditional norms in educational leadership:

> In preparing students and educators for a different future, we need to accept that old paradigms simply do not work anymore for learning leaders in schools. We require a new way of thinking about leadership that calls us to engage in a different conversation with a different emphasis. . . .
>
> Learning leaders need to be conscious of the decisions they make, the way people take on those decisions, and how they support people through those decisions. This consciousness needs to encompass our thoughts, our emotions, and our physical awareness. The preparation work that we do on ourselves, particularly when leading professional learning, leading change, or having conversations with colleagues, needs to be intentional. It is equally important that leaders consider how they view themselves through the process, and what they are cognizant of as they lead themselves and others through any process of change. (Danvers et al., 2021, pp. 14–15)

These early lessons served Michelle well as she moved into her own leadership roles as well as in the work she would eventually do with school leaders. Michelle intentionally supports leaders in developing awareness around their own decision making and the impact that these decisions inevitably have on others.

REFLECTION QUESTIONS

Reflect on the following questions.

- What are internal factors that have made your life positive?
- What do you need to feel satisfied and successful?
- What are you willing to be flexible with? What are your non-negotiables? How do you know?

Establishing Boundaries

Many people avoid confrontation out of fear or discomfort. The result is often a feeling of being trapped in an untenable situation with no viable options to escape. But that is infrequently the case, as options abound for the leader who knows her worth. For example, Michelle realized that she could speak up about other people's expectations of her, and she established limits to ensure that her colleagues understood and honored her needs. One year of being overworked and subjected to unfair expectations was enough for Michelle. Intuiting that something wasn't right, she confronted her principal. She had a secret weapon when she walked into his office the second time: her willingness to resign. By establishing this boundary for herself and communicating it to her principal, she reclaimed control over her decisions.

Educational institutions are replete with a necessary give and take. Educators often take on a little more for the benefit of the students or the program. However, as women, we don't always recognize that we can contribute to defining how things go instead of passively accepting the dynamics set for us by others. Yes, that sometimes means incurring risk, as Michelle did when she resigned from that first job. Shouldering such risks is a *must* for women who understand the paramount importance of asserting their needs and maintaining authenticity. Psychologist and researcher Joaquín Selva (2021) explains, "Setting boundaries is an important part of establishing one's identity and is a crucial aspect of mental health and well-being." Boundaries not only contribute to a person's own sense of self and understanding of self-worth, but they also increase self-confidence by giving one permission to define their own limits. Establishing boundaries is an essential element of creating trust. When a leader shows no boundaries, it can leave employees guessing and wondering. It is important to articulate what the limits are in situations so there is no guessing.

Setting boundaries offers an additional benefit for leaders, protecting them from burnout and supporting them to create an environment suited to their unique strengths. Executive coach Melody Wilding (n.d.) explains why boundaries are essential for women to thrive: "Healthy boundaries at work can make a difference between professional fulfillment or burnout. They are the physical, emotional, and mental limits you create to protect yourself from over-committing, being used, or behaving in unethical ways." Ultimately, boundaries allow us to maintain appropriate control.

Think of a time when you have had to establish clear boundaries in your professional life. Use figure 2.1 (page 32) to reflect on that event. How did you make your message clear? To what extent did it feel confrontational? Why or why not? What was the end result of having set the boundaries? What will you do differently going forward? Next, think of a current situation in your work life where you would benefit from setting clear boundaries. Develop a plan that addresses how you will implement this change.

How I Have Set Boundaries in the Past	
What did I do to make my message clear?	
Did it feel confrontational? Why or why not?	
What happened as a result of setting the boundary?	
What did I learn through the experience?	
How I Plan to Set Boundaries Moving Forward	
What could I do to make my message clear?	
What can I do to feel confident if setting boundaries initiates a confrontation?	
What is one possible outcome of setting a boundary?	
How do I hope this will be different from past experiences of setting boundaries?	

FIGURE 2.1: Worksheet for teasing out boundaries.
*Visit **go.SolutionTree.com/leadership** for a free reproducible version of this figure.*

Valuing Her Worth

As human beings, it's important that we all value the opportunities we get to work and learn. But appreciation should not mean acceptance of being undervalued, particularly with regard to fair compensation. Katie Shonk (2021), a Harvard Business School research associate, notes that a major factor exacerbating the gender pay gap is that men tend to fare better in salary negotiation than women do. Shonk (2021) traces this tendency back to social norms:

> *Deeply ingrained societal gender roles lie at the root of the gender gap in negotiated outcomes. . . . In many cultures, girls are encouraged and expected to be accommodating, concerned with the welfare of others, and relationship-oriented from an early age. Notably, these goals clash with the more assertive behaviors considered to be essential for negotiation success, which is more in line with societal expectations that boys and men be competitive, assertive, and profit oriented. As a result, women may be uncomfortable negotiating forcefully on their behalf.*

What can women do to counteract this tendency? Shonk (2021) suggests that women negotiate more effectively for others than they do for themselves, a traditionally female communal value. Women can harness this trait by recognizing the value they bring to their organization and advocating to be compensated accordingly.

This is exactly what Michelle did. She intuitively knew that the salary she had been initially offered for the position of curriculum director was well beneath the value she brought to the role. Yes, the opportunity provided her tremendous growth and learning, but rather than use that as a way to rationalize a lower salary than the position warranted, she advocated for equity. Do you value your worth, and do you advocate for yourself when the need and opportunity arise?

REFLECTION QUESTIONS

Reflect on the following questions.

- ○ Think about a situation in your life when you knew your worth was undervalued. If you addressed the situation, what steps did you take?

- ○ Name your intuitive knowing around this experience. What might have been the impact had you chosen to ignore your knowing?

- ○ When have you negotiated for something you knew you deserved? How might you extend that skill to other parts of your personal or professional experience?

Food for Thought

In their book *What Works for Women at Work*, authors Joan C. Williams and Rachel Dempsey (2018) identify what they call *tightrope patterns* that women walk daily in the workplace. The tightrope is the fine line that women walk between behaving in traditionally feminine ways in order to meet expectations of colleagues and superiors and behaving in traditionally masculine ways to prove they are as competent as their male coworkers. (We discuss these traits in more detail in chapter 10, page 123.) When women adopt traits that are typically attributed to men, though, the result is not necessarily positive. The often-cited example: an assertive man is considered a "go-getter," whereas an assertive woman is misinterpreted as aggressive and is considered defiant.

This dynamic manifests in a multitude of ways, from minor indignities all the way to unequal pay or the loss of a job. Williams and Dempsey (2018) describe how the gender dynamics they've studied impact women negotiating salaries:

> In a study of people participating in an executive training program, women negotiated $141,643 for their own salaries—but when negotiating for others, the salary figure climbed to $167,250. Why? Two reasons come to mind. One is that women themselves are probably aware, at some level, of the penalty imposed on women for self-promotion—so when negotiating for themselves, they hold back. Even if they don't hold back, the pushback against self-promoting women probably makes woman negotiators less effective when negotiating for themselves than for others. (p. 101)

As natural givers, women often have no trouble at all advocating for others. Finding ways to apply that skill to their own needs is a crucial step in being able to effectively create the needed boundaries that will lead to greater self-worth and self-confidence. Examples abound of women easily standing up for others before themselves, being kinder to others than to themselves, or giving more to others than to themselves. As women find and use their voices to advocate for equity, negotiate salaries, and protect their rights, they are not always received with open arms. Valuing your worth, advocating for fair compensation, and embracing the factors that you have control over are essential to empowered leadership as gender equity continues to evolve.

Conclusion

Michelle's story highlights the themes of developing self-awareness, establishing boundaries, and valuing your worth. She communicated her needs, kept her relationships professional, and created clear structures. Her story offers a model for how to create healthy boundaries at work.

Michelle honored her character, feelings, motives, and desires enough to cultivate the environment that was right for her. Through self-awareness, Michelle improved her listening skills, showed self-control, and increased her creativity. As women listen to their internal selves, build their capacity for self-awareness, and set boundaries to honor their limits, they are empowered to flourish as leaders.

MICHELLE'S LEADERSHIP LESSONS

Developing self-awareness

Establishing boundaries

Valuing her worth

References and Resources

Barroso, A., & Brown, A. (2021, May 25). *Gender pay gap in U.S. held steady in 2020.* Accessed at www.pewresearch.org/fact-tank/2021/05/25/gender-pay-gap-facts on September 15, 2021.

Danvers, J., De Blasio, H., & Grift, G. (2021). *Five ways of being: What learning leaders think, do, and say every day.* Bloomington, IN: Solution Tree Press.

Jacobson, D. A. (2016). *Causes and effects of teacher burnout.* Doctoral dissertation, Walden University, Minneapolis, MN. Accessed at https://scholarworks.waldenu.edu/dissertations/2835 on February 1, 2022.

Selva, J. (2021, February 24). *How to set healthy boundaries: 10 examples + PDF worksheets.* Accessed at https://positivepsychology.com/great-self-care-setting-healthy-boundaries on July 1, 2021.

Shonk, K. (2021, December 21). *Women and negotiation: Narrowing the gender gap in negotiation* [Blog post]. Accessed at www.pon.harvard.edu/daily/business-negotiations/women-and-negotiation-narrowing-the-gender-gap/ on January 10, 2022.

Wilding, M. (n.d.). *How to define healthy boundaries at work* [Blog post]. Accessed at https://melodywilding.com/how-to-define-healthy-boundaries-at-work on August 4, 2021.

Williams, J. C., & Dempsey, R. (2018). *What works for women at work: Four patterns working women need to know.* New York: NYU Press.

CHAPTER 3

On Building Resilience and Finding Courage

*Resilient people . . . possess three characteristics:
a staunch acceptance of reality; a deep belief, often
buttressed by strongly held values, that life is meaningful;
and an uncanny ability to improvise.*

—DIANE COUTU

DEBRA'S STORY
DEBRA E. LANE

Growing up in Texas, I had a serious learning disability. Many summers were spent retaking mathematics classes or getting extra help to prepare for the next school year. Perseverance was my superhero strength. I spent a lot of time studying, and I just never gave up. During my junior year in high school, I took a literacy course, and the English teacher asked me to stay after school one day to talk. She put an article from Newsweek *in front of me and asked me to read the article then synthesize the information back to her. I could not do it; by the time I was on the second paragraph, I could not remember what the first paragraph said. She reached out to my parents and told them to take me to a special dyslexia clinic. She was concerned that my last two years of high school would be too difficult. Her concern was that, given my struggles, there was a distinct possibility that I might face burnout, fail my courses, and not get into college.*

My mom and I went to the clinic, and after seemingly endless rounds of tests, it was confirmed I had dyslexia. It came as a relief to me. I had always felt like I worked harder in school than most of my friends. The next hurdle for me was paying for the clinic. Family circumstances required that I work extra shifts as a cashier at the grocery store to pay for the literacy clinic. After one year attending the clinic, I had made a lot of progress. I met with the owner of the clinic, an eloquent woman who clearly had a vision to help kids like me read and understand the connections literacy could open for me. She sat me down for my review, looked me in the eye, and said, "School will never be easy for you, but you know how to persevere, and perseverance will get you far in life. Don't ever give up!" That day had a lot of impact on my future. I left that clinic feeling proud that I put myself through it financially, proud of sticking with the sessions twice a week for a year, and proud that I had made notable improvements.

Just weeks before I graduated in 1985, a team of teachers cornered me in the library. They wanted to nominate me for a full scholarship to Trinity University in San Antonio if I agreed to be a teacher right then and there. I told them, "Thank you, but no thank you." At the time, I was determined to go into business. My dad was a real estate lawyer, and my mom worked as an office assistant in hospitals and orthodontist offices, having never gone to college. They had the kinds of attitudes about appropriate careers for women that were typical of their generation and often tried to steer my sister and me toward careers in nursing and teaching. But I had bigger plans, and I expected more of myself than that.

The following fall, I attended Baylor University. The general freshmen classes were challenging for me due to the amount of reading assigned. While I managed to get through my first year at Baylor, the outlook began to shift during my second year. I was sitting in my first marketing class in the Hankamer Business School with hundreds of students keen to earn an accounting or marketing degree. I kept tapping my pencil and feeling like something was just not clicking. Here I was, about to start this major in business administration, and I just could not get excited about it. Something was missing.

After her first business class, Debra packed up and went to the Baylor counseling center. Determined to find a major that better suited her, she knew she was going to have to dig deep to identify it. Something inside Debra pulled her toward a move into education, and yet at the same time, she resisted it. She did not want to become a statistic—yet another woman to enter a field that had been traditionally assigned to women. Ultimately, Debra could not deny that what she really wanted was to be for others what the woman at the literacy center had been for her. At the same time, she knew that she wanted to push herself and others beyond traditional constraints of what women could and couldn't do in the 1980s; these two goals—teaching and mentoring—would become intertwined.

After graduating from Baylor with a bachelor's degree in elementary education, I moved to Washington, D.C. While I looked for teaching positions in upper elementary teaching, I waited tables in a small eighteenth century inn near the Central

Intelligence Agency and substitute taught in Fairfax County, Virginia. One day at the inn, I happened to wait on an elementary principal who was looking for an instructional aide. We struck up a conversation and, anxious to get my foot in the door, I jumped at the opportunity to interview. Within two days, I was hired, and just three months later, I became a sixth-grade teacher at a nearby school.

In 1991, my second year of teaching, Fairfax County Public Schools (FCPS) had a generous tuition assistance program. Over time as I worked with students who I knew had similar issues with dyslexia, I recognized ways to adapt my teaching and learning style in the classroom for them. These learning challenges made me a stronger teacher, and I was able to channel my passion for learning into helping others. I applied to Virginia Tech for their curriculum and instruction program for middle school teachers. This program took up time on weekends and weeknights while I continued working at the restaurant in the evenings and taught during the day. After completing the program in a year and a half, I decided to apply to teach overseas. In spite of the fact that my family and friends all thought I was crazy, and I knew very little about what teaching overseas would look like, the thought of living abroad appealed to me, and I signed up for an international job fair. I received offers from international schools in Korea, Egypt, and Singapore. I also learned that FCPS had a partnership with the Carol Morgan School in Santo Domingo, Dominican Republic, and that teaching there would allow me to keep my status with FCPS. This appealed to me. I applied and was hired immediately as a middle school literacy coach.

In the fall of 1994, I moved back to northern Virginia, got married, and took a job as a sixth-grade teacher for students with a range of needs. With up to thirty-six students in the class and little room to move, this proved to be a most challenging year. There was no other recourse but to pull from the innermost depths of my creativity and to think about teaching and learning differently. I experimented with all the traditional parts of the classroom setting—from space utilization to grouping to homework and grading. Somehow, against the odds, I made this situation work for those kids. And my principal noticed.

Despite my success, the approval of my principal and my first master's degree weren't enough to resolve my feelings of inadequacy. I was suffering from imposter syndrome wrapped tightly around overachieving, and so I went back to school, working full time while studying education leadership. I also watched and learned from my principal. She taught me how to grow a team of teachers. She was strategic in how she went about placing teachers. I also learned from her the importance of building a supportive culture in which the team celebrated weddings, births, graduations, and other milestones together, and we were there for one another, building each other up. The clear vision she had for both students and staff was inspiring and made me want to aspire to be that kind of leader.

It was a competitive time to apply for assistant principal positions, but in 1998 I was hired to work in an area of FCPS that had special needs. I worked as an assistant principal at the school for two years, then transferred to another school as an assistant principal, this time at a Gifted and Talented Center school. Each of these experiences helped me grow as a leader. After five years as an assistant principal at a school that served student populations at very different extremes, I moved to a school where the staff knew the principal was retiring and wanted me to serve as his replacement. It was a fabulous school with a high-achieving staff and student population, a hardworking, appreciative community, and an innovative and reflective ethos. Under my leadership, our school was featured in many research articles and journals. Our teachers worked hard; they were risk takers and reflective practitioners. During the next five years, I committed to developing others in the same way my mentors had helped me grow—through conviction, goal setting, self-trust, and commitment.

In 2010, my family moved to Shanghai, where I took on a principal role for Shanghai American School for three years. The school is the largest international school in China and has two campuses for 2,800 K–12 students. Both campuses offer Advanced Placement and IB programs. I became a member of the school's strategic planning committee, was on the school finance committee, and participated in a number of accreditation visits for the Western Association of Schools and Colleges. In my time as a learning leader, I have watched other leaders closely to learn from their experiences. I have learned to listen keenly, especially in the first year in any position.

Communities need time to build trust and empathy with a new leader. By listening to the people around you, you understand and interpret the messages they are providing around your own growth. Ultimately, we do not rise alone, and we need the support of others—whether that be in the form of strong leadership, supportive colleagues, or mentors. But as crucial as such support is, leaders also need the resilience and courage to persevere in the face of obstacles, even when our most staunch supporters can't always be there for us. My aspiration is to be a head of school in the future. How we educate children has to change, and I want to be part of that change.

Debra's story highlights the power of building resilience, honoring her instincts, choosing persistence, and leading with humility. Debra was able to identify early on what it was that motivated her, and she stayed true to her goal. She trusted herself enough to follow her dreams, and in spite of the barriers that appeared along the way, she persisted. Her story took her in some surprising directions because of her commitment and tenacity. In this chapter, you'll look closely at the lessons Debra learned and reflect on how these qualities inform your experiences as a leader.

Leadership Lessons

The path to leadership is complex and takes many turns. Debra proved countless times that she could take on just about anything thrown at her and make it work. She put herself through school, earning degree upon degree while working full time, getting married, and starting a family. Debra's path to leadership wasn't easy, but she exhibited certain traits that made her success possible. Let's examine the lessons Debra learned along the way and imagine the role that resilience and courage play on your path to leadership.

Building Resilience

Debra faced the persistent challenge presented by her dyslexia during her education. But she never allowed that to become a barrier to pursuing her dreams. The experiences of studying harder than her peers, receiving her diagnosis, and working to pay for the literacy clinic taught Debra to persevere and helped her develop the resilience she needed to keep pursuing her dreams of making a difference in the lives of others.

Women who lead need great reserves of resilience in order to persist through the unexpected challenges that come with any leadership role as well as the barriers (many of which we describe throughout this book) that come with leading as women. Executive coach Monique Valcour (2017) notes that a resilient leader:

- Has a clear sense of purpose
- Demonstrates progress
- Recognizes others' efforts
- Exhibits compassion for self and others
- Forms meaningful connections with others

Without necessarily knowing this was what she was doing, Debra embraced each of these principles throughout her career. Resilience is the leadership lesson that stands out above all else in Debra's story as a result of her purpose and persistence.

REFLECTION QUESTIONS

Reflect on the following questions.

- Identify someone in your life with great resilience. What are the traits that person exhibits that contribute to their resilience?

- Reflect for a moment on Valcour's principles of resilience. When have you exhibited some or all of these principles? How might these have contributed to your ability to overcome challenges?

- How can you become more resilient?

Honoring Her Instincts

Even in high school, Debra's teachers saw something in her that she did not yet see. Determined to move beyond traditional gender roles that expect women to become nurses or teachers, Debra took a detour through the study of business, only to realize that this was not her calling. Making that decision required Debra to have a tremendous amount of trust in the voices of her mentors, but even more than that, trust in herself. Debra learned to trust her instincts, and once she did, things began to move quickly from there. In just a few short years, Debra had a bachelor's degree and two master's degrees and was on her way into educational leadership.

In order to trust their instincts, leaders must be self-aware, clear about their purpose, and willing to make decisions that support their chosen path. Biologically and psychologically, instinct refers to behavior that is performed without thought and is related to survival. Instinct, however, is connected to environmental and social factors, and is the direct result of learning (Yirka, 2017). This means that a person's instincts will change based on their experiences.

Instinct alone, though, is not enough to justify decision making. When combined with rational or analytical thought, instinct can produce successful outcomes (Bonabeau, 2003; Corrado, 2018). When women trust in their instincts by using intuition as a starting place for decision making, they are honoring their experiences, lessons learned, and expertise developed over time. Honoring one's instinct means being willing to learn from the past. It also means overcoming self-doubt.

Think of a time when you second-guessed a decision you made. Can you point to factors that led to your lack of self-trust? Figure 3.1 asks you to name an event where you can identify that self-trust was absent or present and to reflect on the implications. What resulted from your actions during the event? How might your ability or inability to trust yourself have impacted the outcome? What do you wish to do differently in the future?

REFLECTION QUESTIONS

Reflect on the following questions.

○ How have your experiences and the lessons you have learned impacted your decision-making process over time?

○ What role does instinct play in your professional life?

○ Reflect on a time when trusting your instincts did not produce the desired outcome. What was missing?

Event	
Was self-trust present or absent?	
What was the result of my actions?	
What might have happened if my relationship to self-trust had been different?	
What might I do differently next time?	

FIGURE 3.1: Worksheet for teasing out self-trust.

Visit **go.SolutionTree.com/leadership** *for a free reproducible version of this figure.*

Choosing Persistence

Debra identified early on that her superhero strength was persistence and was made possible because she was committed to her objective. Debra's entire professional life can be characterized by commitment: to her goals, to her values, to her growth, to herself, and to others. In listening carefully to others and being willing to learn from them, Debra demonstrated to her teachers that she was committed to them not just as professionals, but also as people.

The ability to persist in the face of challenge, stay true to one's goals, and recover from failure is paramount to the success of any leader. Leaders foster innovation, drive change, resolve conflict, and navigate crises. Consider the impact of COVID-19. School leaders around the world have persisted in order to push through the many challenges posed by the pandemic. Leaders couldn't walk away during the crisis; they poured all of their energy and focus into continued learning and community well-being.

According to psychologist and coach Ben Dean (n.d.), the key to developing persistence is the existence of challenge: "just as fear is a prerequisite for courage, challenge is a prerequisite for perseverance." In other words, in order to develop persistence (or its synonym, perseverance), one must get into the habit of tackling hard tasks. Leaders can step outside of their comfort zone and take small risks to build the kind of stamina needed to persist through the hard times. And the habit of building persistence begins early on. Clearly, Debra's early exposure to challenge in school formed the building blocks for the persistence she would exhibit later in life.

REFLECTION QUESTIONS

Reflect on the following questions.

○ Describe an example of when commitment made something possible in your life that might otherwise have been unlikely.

○ Reflect on some of the risks you took or challenges you faced earlier in your life. How might these have contributed to the persistence you have today?

○ How might you continue to practice persistence?

Leading With Humility

Leadership is not for the faint of heart, and while it may seem obvious the important role courage has in being an effective leader, too many leaders fail to understand the importance of humility. Humble leaders have the courage to bring people together, celebrate them as humans, listen to them, think outside of the box, create opportunities for others, and make the difficult decisions. Throughout Debra's life, she pulled from the reserves of her commitment and courage to succeed. Humility is not to be confused with lack of confidence. In fact, it is the person who lacks confidence that also lacks humility.

Debra's commitment to learning and leading learning required that she be constantly reflective and determined to grow. She sought to serve her students and colleagues, putting them at the core of her purpose. Emotional intelligence expert Harvey Deutschendorf (2021) calls this *servant leadership*: "humble, collaborative, and driven by the well-being of the staff and the organization's service of the greater good."

Servant leadership might sound good in theory, but is it effective? In his article "Why Humble Leaders Make the Best Leaders," author and recruiter Jeff Hyman (2018) suggests that humility is a leadership superpower and that humble leaders "listen more effectively, inspire great teamwork and focus everyone (including themselves) on organizational goals better than leaders who don't score high on humility." Ultimately, humility comes from the knowledge that we have more to learn, along with the commitment to continue along the path of personal growth. Being humble does not mean that a person has to deny their self-worth, but rather it honors the fact that everyone brings real strengths to the table. Humility is the recognition that we can do more together than we can do alone.

REFLECTION QUESTIONS

Reflect on the following questions.

- To what extent does humility, compassion, or service play a role in your own leadership?

- When has humility opened doors for you as a leader that had been previously closed?

- Think about a team of colleagues you work with and reflect on each member's individual strengths. What unique aspect does each of you contribute to the team's overall effectiveness? How might you celebrate those strengths?

Food for Thought

Katty Kay and Claire Shipman, authors of the 2009 book *Womenomics*, published an article called "The Confidence Gap" in *The Atlantic* in 2014. The article begins:

> *For years, we women have kept our heads down and played by the rules. We've been certain that with enough hard work, our natural talents would be recognized and rewarded.*

We've made undeniable progress. In the United States, women now earn more college and graduate degrees than men do. We make up half the workforce, and we are closing the gap in middle management. Half a dozen global studies, conducted by the likes of Goldman Sachs and Columbia University, have found that companies employing women in large numbers outperform their competitors on every measure of profitability. Our competence has never been more obvious.

That's all amazing, except that women continue to be outnumbered in leadership positions in all industries, including education. Kay and Shipman (2014) attribute this to women's lack of confidence. They saw evidence of this in a review of Hewlett-Packard's personnel records, which found that women at HP tended not to apply for promotions they were clearly qualified for unless they met 100 percent of the preferred qualifications on the job description, whereas men at HP applied if they met 60 percent of the requirements. Ultimately, then, upper-level openings are being filled by men who are less qualified but more confident. As women, we build confidence by listening to our instincts, building resilience, and honoring ourselves. As we cultivate these qualities and build confidence, everyone in the workplace benefits.

Conclusion

Humility in leadership feeds overall effectiveness of an organization, a truth illustrated in Debra's leadership style. Being willing to admit mistakes, share credit, and learn from others made her an effective leader. She learned to trust her instincts and channel her ambition back into the organizations she worked for or projects she managed, rather than use it for personal gain. Her ability to build resilience, trust her instincts, and choose persistence has strengthened her professional relationships and determined the trajectory of her career. Her motto, "You will only get better in life by failing at things, learning from those experiences, and moving on" has grounded her along the way.

DEBRA'S LEADERSHIP LESSONS

Building resilience

Honoring her instincts

Choosing persistence

Leading with humility

References and Resources

Bonabeau, E. (2003). Don't trust your gut. *Harvard Business Review*. Accessed at https://hbr.org/2003/05/dont-trust-your-gut on November 29, 2021.

Cameron, J. (2016). *The artist's way: A spiritual path to higher creativity*. New York: Penguin Publishing Group.

Corrado, M. E. (2018, June 26). *Can intuition play a role in effective decision making?* Accessed at www.aseonline.org/News/Articles/ArtMID/628/ArticleID/1523/Can-Intuition-Play-a-Role-in-Effective-Decision-Making on November 29, 2021.

Dean, B. (n.d.). *Persistence defined*. Accessed at www.authentichappiness.sas.upenn.edu/newsletters/authentichappinesscoaching/persistence on November 29, 2021.

Deutschendorf, H. (2021, January 20). 7 reasons humility is a highly desired leadership trait. *Fast Company*. Accessed at www.fastcompany.com/90595756/7-reasons-humility-is-a-highly-desired-leadership-trait on August 24, 2021.

Hyman, J. (2018, October 31). Why humble leaders make the best leaders. *Forbes*. Accessed at www.forbes.com/sites/jeffhyman/2018/10/31/humility/?sh=5e68b1e81c80 on July 19, 2021.

Kay, K., & Shipman, C. (2014, May). The confidence gap. *The Atlantic*. Accessed at www.theatlantic.com/magazine/archive/2014/05/the-confidence-gap/359815/ on July 19, 2021.

Valcour, M. (2017, September 28). What we can learn about resilience from female leaders of the UN. *Harvard Business Review*. Accessed at https://hbr.org/2017/09/what-we-can-learn-about-resilience-from-female-leaders-of-the-un on November 29, 2021.

Williams, J. C., & Dempsey, R. (2018). *What works for women at work: Four patterns working women need to know*. New York: NYU Press.

Yirka, B. (2017, April 7). *Biology professors suggest instincts evolved from learning*. Accessed at https://phys.org/news/2017-04-biology-professors-instincts-evolved.html on November 29, 2021.

CHAPTER 4

On Overcoming Imposter Syndrome and Transcending Titles

The universe falls in with worthy plans.

—Julia Cameron

Kim's Story
Kimberly Cullen

I am a profound believer that things happen for a reason. My children laugh uncomfortably at my theory that there is a great energy that guides the universe, but I shrug my shoulders and say, "You watch." I believe in synchronicity, that things fall into place when they are supposed to and that, yes, you can make things happen. Somehow, the things that are supposed to come about find their way in. See, I never planned to get into education, much less leadership. I was going to be a doctor. I knew that from the age of eight. I would be a small-town family doctor, I would marry a man who drove a pickup truck, and I would have my own practice. We would have seven children, live on a ranch, and have horses. These were the visions of a young girl who lived in Texas. Moving to Spain when I was nine threw a few kinks in those plans.

I was "good at school," did well academically, was liked by my teachers, and had the confidence to play sports and be on the student council. But going to college away from home and facing repeated setbacks killed my confidence. I eventually abandoned the idea of going to medical school, opting instead for a major in religious studies. After college, I found myself back home in Madrid trying to figure out what to do with my life. As luck would have it, I was offered a job filing papers in the headmaster's office at my old school. Back in the safety of the very campus where I had thrived, I felt renewed hope. So, with the encouragement of my boss, I went back to school, aiming to get a master's degree in special education.

Deciding to stay closer to home, I didn't go all the way back to the United States. Instead, I decided to stay close to family and went to the United Kingdom, hoping for a much easier transition than in college. But it wasn't all it was cracked up to be. I found out after arriving on campus that this particular degree required me to be a qualified teacher, which I was not. So instead of an MEd, I would get an MA, and on top of that, it would not be in special education, but rather in education of the hearing impaired. When I look back, I wonder why I wasn't aware of these facts when I applied, but there I was, already in the UK and starting my program. These were huge setbacks that challenged my very notion of the future, and I wasn't equipped to handle the disappointment. For months, I hoped to wake up in the morning and think to myself, "Ah, YES! There is my future. That's why I'm here." It never happened. In fact, the moment when it all might have come together—the first time I got to work with students in the classroom as a teacher—I panicked. Knowing that my colleagues were all qualified teachers and I was not, I became paralyzed by fear. The "what ifs" overwhelmed me: What if I had nothing to say? What if the kids were smarter than me? What if they laughed? What if they realized I had no idea what I was doing? Wait. What if I tried and failed, and then teaching was out of the picture, too? Then what? That terrified me more than anything.

As I realized that my colleagues and I would observe one another, I made myself sick with worry. I stood outside the classroom door, feeling like I would throw up at any moment. I couldn't make myself go in. Instead, I turned around and walked out. I went back to my dorm, stayed in bed for several days, and pretty much waited out the rest of the school year. I immersed myself in research for my dissertation, occasionally met my brother for lunch, and allowed myself to be enveloped by dark clouds and the persistent English drizzle. I developed a deeply layered depression, and by spring, I was experiencing a resurgence of the anorexia that had appeared early on in college.

Kim finished her degree, more from a sense of obligation than passion. As soon as she was able, she returned to Madrid, degree in hand, and went back to the school hoping to find work. As chance would have it, the school hoped to build an alumni program, so the head hired Kim to take on this work. With a strong work ethic and a desire to please, Kim did her work exceptionally well and, after two years, was promoted to development head.

Promotions are double-edged swords. The reward for doing something well is doing something new. Suddenly, I found myself doing a job that was unfamiliar and challenging. And while I knew that I could learn, the challenge was in convincing others that I knew what I was doing from the start. I remember going out to dinner early on in my new position and being introduced to a parent from the school. When he asked me what I did, and I answered that I was the development head, he looked at me quizzically and said, "Oh, yeah? And what exactly do you develop?" I had no idea what I developed, and I resented him for asking. I knew that it involved fundraising, creating relationships, and planning events. I also knew that, as an introvert, I found all of that terrifying.

Not wanting to feel like a fraud, I became a quick learner. I was organized, a good communicator, and I was also honest. I never pretended to be outgoing, and I never tried to be a salesperson. My gift was in the ability to give an honest and eloquent voice to the things that I thought, felt, and knew. That meant that I could talk all day long about my school and all it had to offer. That honest voice allowed me to create meaningful relationships with parents—even the difficult ones. I could take the feistiest parents and enlist their help in something that was important to them, and as a result, I could help them transform a little of that negative energy into a positive outcome. Organizing the events at school allowed me to help people identify and capitalize on their interests and strengths. It was something that I was good at, something I enjoyed. I knew there was more I needed to do and learn. While working with parents was helpful and meaningful, I really wanted to work with young people. My boss, the same one who encouraged me to get my first master's degree, suggested I think about high school counseling. And so, I enrolled in an online master's program in counseling.

The counseling program was comprehensive, but it had a fatal flaw. Because there was no residency component to this particular program, the focus was theory-based, and I would not become a licensed counselor. Sound familiar? I was learning, though, to trade that woe-is-me outlook for a bring-it-on attitude. I got straight As in my program. After three years, I got a master of science in human services with a specialization in counseling studies—and in the moment, it made no difference to me that I wasn't a licensed counselor. I was a full-time professional woman with three children (yes, I had a third baby while studying), and I had just gotten a second master's degree. As it happened, the high school counselor at the school decided well past recruiting season that he would be leaving the following year. That meant the school had to scramble to find a counselor late in the season. My boss encouraged me to apply for the job, so I did. For the next six years, I was the high school guidance and college counselor.

As Kim took on each new job, she realized there was little room for error. She had to get it right from the start despite the feelings of inadequacy that surfaced each time she held a new title. It took Kim several years to "feel like a counselor." And yet, she pushed forward. What emerged as a strength for Kim was her belief in herself, regardless of the title. In the early days of her work as a counselor, Kim felt like a fraud when she would identify herself with the title. She felt no more like a counselor than she had a teacher of the deaf or a development head. But her experience told her each new situation would stretch her beyond imagination, and not only would she learn, she would grow.

Being a counselor turned out to be a perfect intersection of my strengths, and it was the first time in my adult life that I began to feel called to a profession. I was needed and useful; I was making a difference. And at the same time, I was growing as an adult and as a woman. When you combine purpose, success, and confidence, and you add a little recognition and appreciation, you end up with the perfect recipe for promotion. It was only natural, given my path so far, that I would be offered the chance to try out a new role.

When I was promoted to dean of students, I had the option to say no. My husband and I talked about it at length. Saying no meant that I would continue to go to work every day to do something I loved, for kids I adored. Saying yes meant that I would move into the complex world of school administration, and there was no guarantee that I would like it or be good at it. But saying yes also meant opening a window to opportunities I hadn't previously considered. The shift from counselor to dean was a tough one. Because I was now responsible for discipline in addition to supporting the administration, it didn't matter that I was the same person and same professional with all of the same qualities and strengths. Dean of students became my master status, and that meant that overnight, I became the bad cop. Students who had told me their greatest secrets only a few months before suddenly avoided making eye contact with me.

Each of my previous transitions had presented its share of challenges. Mostly, however, the challenges revolved around learning more, doing more, growing into the position. As I adjusted to each new role, I felt a tangible growth in my professional capacity. This was different, though. I thought that becoming a disciplinarian meant I could no longer do the parts I had gotten good at . . . until I met Maria. Maria was a sophomore who didn't like the rules. She was angry at a world that told her who and how to be. She didn't hurt anyone or break any laws, but she made sure she pushed the boundaries—all of them—just enough to be noticed. And it meant that she spent a lot of time in my office. Maria, with her sweatpants and short green hair, was cooler and smarter and kinder than most other kids. But she was different from most other kids. Popularity in the traditional sense escaped her. Most traditional things escaped her, and this made her both mad and apathetic. Maria needed more than just a dean. Working with her helped me realize that I could be both a counselor and a disciplinarian. It didn't matter what position I held or what job I was asked to do—I finally understood my place. I strived to be someone who cared about people, what they thought about themselves, how they interpreted their place in the world, and what they got out of their experiences. This was the beginning of my transition to leadership.

Almost ten years after I became the dean of students and five years into my most recent role of upper school director, I think about the headmaster who convinced me to get a master's degree in education. I have learned that titles don't make leaders—leadership makes leaders. And leadership itself is a means, not an end. As such, leadership looks different in different people and in different roles, and it is in a constant process of renewal. I don't know where this road will take me, but as I consider the possibilities, I will find myself again and again in that familiar place, preparing to take on new challenges I can't quite define and ones I know I haven't faced before. I look back, though, and realize that the bricks were laid early on. And when I consider what I have learned, the path ahead isn't quite as scary.

In this chapter, we'll look closely at the lessons Kim learned on her journey to educational leadership. By believing in herself, embracing failure, and having faith in purpose, she moved beyond her self-doubt and found the courage to lead from her authentic self. Sometimes, a person's perception of what leadership should be contrasts with the leadership strengths they present. This can happen easily for women when they are surrounded by male leaders. When Kim recognized that she did not have to change who she was, she began to lead authentically. As you read the lessons and questions in the following paragraphs, reflect on how these qualities inform your experiences as a leader.

Leadership Lessons

Kim learned some powerful lessons along her journey through education into leadership. The keys to her success: learning by doing, intersecting her strengths, taking full advantage of opportunities, and growing around her learning. Kim grew her repertoire of skills throughout her career. She knew that to become an effective leader she had to keep mastering new competencies instead of relying on a limited set of her natural capabilities.

Kim recognized that her daily responsibilities and challenges required her to learn on the job. Growing as a leader often happens as you draw lessons and insights from difficult experiences and apply the new knowledge and skills you learned through the process.

Believing in Herself

After Kim received her promotion, she struggled to feel competent in her new and unfamiliar role. But she found her path forward by committing to be a fast learner and leaning into her unique gifts. In moments when we feel like a fraud or are overwhelmed by a host of new tasks, it's tempting to doubt our capabilities, to fear that we don't have what it takes. But Kim's story demonstrates how trust in the growth process and unwavering belief in oneself can carry a leader through challenging times.

A drive to be perfect, to avoid mistakes, and to limit risks is just one of the many barriers women experience on the journey of professional empowerment. This struggle to believe in themselves often keeps women out of the running for leadership positions. Writer and executive coach Gill Corkindale (2008) says that *imposter syndrome* is at the root of this experience, defining it as "a collection of feelings of inadequacy that persist despite evident success." Corkindale (2008) goes on to say:

> *"Imposters" suffer from chronic self-doubt and a sense of intellectual fraudulence that override any feelings of success or external proof of their competence. They seem unable to internalize their accomplishments, however successful they are in their field. High achieving, highly successful people often suffer, so imposter syndrome doesn't equate with low self-esteem or a lack of self-confidence. In fact, some researchers have linked it with perfectionism, especially in women and among academics.*

Though Kim was well acquainted with imposter syndrome, she didn't allow it to sideline her. Instead, she pushed through her self-doubt, sensing that, regardless of the title, the responsibility, or the role, she was competent. She knew that she could learn and trusted that she would gain the skills she needed with time, commitment, and practice. Within the context of an international school environment, with expectant eyes watching her and discerning parents ready to judge, there was little room for error. So she told herself "I can" and, ultimately, she did.

REFLECTION QUESTIONS

Reflect on the following questions.

○ Think about a time when you were in a new or unfamiliar role. Were you able to access belief in yourself? How did that impact your ability to grow into that role?

○ Do you experience imposter syndrome? What coping strategies do you rely on to push through it?

○ If you're currently struggling with self-doubt, what are three practical steps you could take right now to trust in the growth process and believe in your ability to rise to the challenge?

Think back to a time in your life when you had an opportunity to do something that you didn't feel prepared or qualified to do. Use figure 4.1 (page 56) to identify moments when you have exhibited courage in the face of a challenge or were unable to do so. How did you respond to the challenge? Why did you decide to move forward or back down? In hindsight, how might you have responded differently? How might the outcome have been different?

As you reflect on your own answers to the questions in figure 4.1, take yourself out of the equation and instead think of what you would say to a close friend who didn't believe in herself. Chances are, you will feel much more generous in how you approach a friend. So next, have that same conversation with yourself as though you were your friend.

Embracing Failure

Kim's story shows how fear of failure can be paralyzing. In a moment when she had the chance to shine, fear sent her into hiding. Through those difficult experiences, Kimberly learned that she would not achieve her goals by playing it safe. It was through taking the risk that she would grow. Being willing to take risks requires courage. It means understanding that failure is a real possibility.

Women often strive to avoid failure, to do everything right the first time. Fearing they might be seen as incompetent, they don't take risks. As women, we may hold ourselves to unrealistic standards because we believe something is innately wrong with us when we fail; a shift in mindset may be helpful to interrupt this pattern. Psychologist Carol Dweck (2007) writes about failure through the lens of growth mindset versus fixed mindset. A *growth mindset* allows people to accept failure more readily because they view their traits as constantly under development, whereas a *fixed mindset* keeps people stuck in the feedback loop of poor self-confidence because they believe they're either good at something or they're not (Dweck, 2007). By challenging ourselves to persevere and choosing to embrace failure as a path to growth, we set ourselves up for greater success.

REFLECTION QUESTIONS

Reflect on the following questions.

- Recall a time in your life when you took a risk, knowing it might lead to failure. How did you feel as you made the decision to take the risk?

- How did you feel during? How did you feel afterward?

- If you haven't identified yourself as courageous, why not? How might embracing a growth mindset allow you to become courageous?

Event	
How did I respond to the challenge?	
Did I face the challenge? Why or why not?	
If I could have a do-over, what might I do differently?	
What might the new outcome be?	

FIGURE 4.1: Worksheet for teasing out courage.

*Visit **go.SolutionTree.com/leadership** for a free reproducible version of this figure.*

Having Faith in Purpose

Kim noted her belief that things happen for a reason. As an optimist, she believed that if she was faced with a challenge, then there was a reason for it. And if she passed up an opportunity, there was probably a good reason for that, too. She wasted little time on regret, understanding that life is unpredictable and sometimes unfair, and as humans, the greatest choice we have is in how we approach the challenges that come our way. The reason, then, is ours to decide.

Writing for *Discover*, journalist Amy Paturel (2019) reports that when it comes to explaining uncanny coincidences in life, "the majority of scientists say it's simple mathematics . . . such scenarios are part of our brain's innate need to create order out of chaos—and we experience them more often when we're paying attention." But psychiatrist Carl Jung found the phenomenon of persistent coincidences compelling, exploring the idea through his synchronicity theory (Vernon, 2011). Jung described *synchronicity* as the simultaneous occurrence of two seemingly unrelated things that have a meaningful connection. How or whether we make meaning from these experiences is a personal and highly subjective experience. But, as Kim illustrated, finding meaning in the synchronicities of life can act as a spotlight to illuminate the path ahead of us in moments of uncertainty and self-doubt.

REFLECTION QUESTIONS

Reflect on the following questions.

○ Reflect on a particular moment in your life when things came together in a way that you couldn't explain—when a window closed and a door opened. What lessons did you take from that moment?

○ How does synchronicity connect with leadership?

○ How can you learn to embrace these moments more openly with acceptance, grace, gratitude?

Food for Thought

A report by McKinsey & Company (2019), "Women in the Workplace 2019," aims to help companies create greater equity in the workplace by reporting on the state of women in corporate America. The report discusses topics from how women navigate the corporate ladder, to the kinds of workplace culture they encounter, to instituting practices for increased diversity. In particular, it notes the barriers women face to stepping into senior positions:

Progress at the top is constrained by a broken rung. The biggest obstacle women face on the path to senior leadership is at the first step up to manager. For every 100 men promoted to and hired as manager, only 72 women are promoted and hired. This broken rung results in more women getting stuck at the entry level and fewer women becoming managers. Not surprisingly, men end up holding 62 percent of manager-level positions, while women hold just 38 percent.

This early inequality has a long-term impact on the talent pipeline. Since men significantly outnumber women at the manager level, there are significantly fewer women to hire or promote to senior managers. The number of women decreases at every subsequent level. So even as hiring and promotion rates improve for women at senior levels, women as a whole can never catch up. There are simply too few women to advance. (McKinsey & Company, 2019)

That early discrepancy has a magnifying effect by the time we look at senior-level positions. Alison Cook, Alicia R. Ingersoll, and Christy Glass (2020) point to a mechanism they've termed the *glass cliff*: "The glass cliff suggests that women are more likely than men to be appointed to top leadership positions in organizations that are struggling, in crisis or at risk to fail." Highly qualified White men don't want to take these jobs as the positions are risky with a high chance of failure, so they're often given to women. There are women succeeding and failing in these perilous positions. The women that are succeeding are women like Kim, who have tried many different jobs, learned along the way, and have a strong sense of purpose.

Conclusion

Kim's story highlights the power of believing in oneself, embracing failure, and having faith in purpose. Despite paralyzing fear and feelings of being an imposter, Kim pushed through self-doubt to achieve the goals she set for herself. When women know they are capable and worthy, when they keep their eyes on their strengths and determine to grow beyond their weaknesses, they have begun the journey to success.

KIM'S LEADERSHIP LESSONS
Believing in herself
Embracing failure
Having faith in purpose

References and Resources

Cook, A., Ingersoll, A. R., & Glass, C. (2020, March). *The glass cliff.* Accessed at http://my.aasa.org/AASA/Resources/SAMag/2020/Mar20/Cook.aspx on August 6, 2021.

Corkindale, G. (2008). Overcoming imposter syndrome. *Harvard Business Review.* Accessed at https://hbr.org/2008/05/overcoming-imposter-syndrome on August 5, 2021.

Dweck, C. S. (2007). *Mindset: The new psychology of success.* New York: Ballantine Books.

Kagan, J. (2021, April 9). *Glass cliff.* Accessed at www.investopedia.com/terms/g/glass-cliff.asp on July 19, 2021.

Lesley University. (n.d.). *Perception is reality: The looking-glass self.* Accessed at www.lesley.edu/article/perception-is-reality-the-looking-glass-self on July 19, 2021.

McKinsey & Company. (2019). *Women in the workplace 2019.* New York: Author. Accessed at https://wiw-report.s3.amazonaws.com/Women_in_the_Workplace_2019.pdf on July 19, 2021.

Paturel, A. (2019, January 2). The science behind coincidence. *Discover.* Accessed at www.discovermagazine.com/mind/the-science-behind-coincidence on August 6, 2021.

Rose, T., & Ogas, O. (2020). *Dark horse: Achieving success through the pursuit of fulfillment.* San Francisco: HarperOne.

Sandberg, S. (2015). *Lean in: Women, work, and the will to lead.* London: Random House.

Vernon, M. (2011, July 4). *Carl Jung, part 6: Synchronicity.* Accessed at www.theguardian.com/commentisfree/2011/jul/04/carl-jung-synchronicity on October 26, 2021.

CHAPTER 5

On Getting Unstuck and Redefining Success

*The most notable fact that culture imprints
on women [is] the sense of our limits.
The most important thing one woman can do for
another is to illuminate her actual possibilities.*

—ADRIENNE RICH

ALEASHA'S STORY
ALEASHA MORRIS

I have never let myself truly experience the joys of my success. In fact, even writing the words my success *feels counter to the message of humble ambition that I've choked on my entire life. I was taught to think about myself in ways that don't always align with reality. So, despite years of evidence to the contrary, I didn't see myself as someone who made success happen. Rather than acknowledging my successes as the cumulative output of my efforts, I felt each accomplishment was utterly disconnected from the previous one, as though each individual achievement was the result of a little merit and a lot of luck. I stayed focused, pursuing each new step, level, degree, whatever it was, convinced it was necessary for my advancement in the field of education. Each new certification or title was wrapped up in a vicious cycle of desire to achieve, chased by self-doubt and anxiety about the outcome, and then silent relief that I pulled it off—but never, ever joy. As an adult, I realized that I had spent most of my life terrified of the real success that I had been striving for because it was so closely linked to the near-miss of failure that it should only be whispered about in my mind, as if speaking it out loud would somehow jinx the result or cast a shadow over my luck.*

School was easy and natural for me. Perhaps that's why I never strayed too far from the familiar rhythm. My parents were first-generation university graduates and educators. Options for career advancement were limited in those days, so we moved around a lot so that my dad could climb the proverbial ladder. For a Canadian public school educator in the 1980s, this meant moving from one small town to the next, going from teacher to vice principal to principal and eventually the pinnacle of leadership, superintendent. Climbing each new rung on the ladder meant that we had to pack up and find our own way in the next town. What I didn't realize at the time was that my dad's career path was deeply entwined with his hope of giving his children more opportunities to succeed than he'd ever had. The bigger the town, the bigger the possibility for us all. So, from very early on, I saw that failure was not an option, and the stops along the way were simply a means to an end.

My parents taught me to work hard, be kind, and try everything. As children of depression-era parents, they were never effusive in their praise, but they encouraged me to be my best, take opportunities, put in the work . . . but always have a backup plan—just in case. The subtle messaging was to be the best at whatever I set out to do but always be prepared for failure in order to mitigate any potential emotional or financial disaster. And so, I learned how to play it safe rather than follow my instinct, which often seemed radical or even reckless in comparison. Afraid that even the most fleeting celebration might be overshadowed by failure, oozing its way through the cracks to reveal that any success was a mirage, I never dwelled on my accomplishments. Instead, I quickly moved on, trying to prove to myself that I was capable of dodging the inevitable blow of failure. Unfortunately, by avoiding it for so long, I was woefully unprepared the first time it happened to me. I remember it vividly: wanting desperately to go to law school but falling short of the score I needed on the LSAT. For me, it was an epic fail, and having never experienced failure, I didn't know how to turn it around. Since not succeeding had never been an option, I didn't know how to pick myself back up, to try again. The disappointment was so great that I couldn't find the resolve I needed to keep moving forward. I lacked grit, resilience, confidence.

With no clear plan B, law school was out. So I leaned on the only backup plan I could think of: diving into education. I worked hard, got all of the right qualifications and degrees, did my jobs well, and was eventually on a leadership path. But I fell into the same trap that many talented women fall into. In international schools, aspiring, ambitious women were at the mercy of a limited number of titled leadership roles within a school. With so much potential and no place to go, women like myself had to leave and get their leadership start in another school, earn yet another degree to add to their long list of certifications to prove their credibility and commitment to the pursuit, or wait patiently while stuffing their ambition away so as not to draw attention to the fact that they would dare to leave the classroom. At one point, I also felt like these were my only options. I was stuck. I had no one to process my choices with, and the answers in conventional wisdom always seemed to prevail. Although that wisdom had been enough for many years, I had a nagging feeling that this wasn't supposed to be my path. I needed something more.

A common theme among the stories of women who aspire to leadership roles is the sense that they need to continually prove themselves by gaining additional qualifications, studying more, or serving in a job that traditionally represents a precursor to a leadership role. If one must be qualified, how much is enough? Endlessly pursuing qualification hints at perfectionism, and the perfectionist trait is common in aspiring women leaders. If we must be perfect, the criteria will never be enough. And striving for perfection, women tend to take fewer risks that might ultimately land them leadership roles.

I eventually took my first small step in a slightly different direction beyond the classroom, accepting a position as school counselor at the Singapore American School in 2006. There was a fine line between counseling children and coaching adults, and around this time, I found myself regularly reaching out to others when they needed someone to connect with. I realized that I had a knack for guiding others through their own life challenges and that this was something I wanted to expand on. My struggles to figure out which professional path I should take had not been in vain after all.

While I was still in Singapore working as a counselor, I stretched my professional wings a bit and began to combine my experience and credentials to create something new: I built a practice working with educational leaders, supporting them in critical yet undervalued intersections of their professional and personal development. I wanted to agitate their thinking, compel them toward their goals, and lift them into their potential. What I did not know at the time was how deeply the stories of the women I coached would affect me and how profoundly their struggles would reflect my own. While our contexts are incredibly diverse, the issues women face—from the institutionalized favoring of men in leadership roles, to the need to be perfect, strong, and capable of doing everything at once, to the self-inflicted barriers that arise from those issues—are indeed universal. And soon, I realized how my internal narrative was contributing to the lifelong tension I'd always felt between my ambition and my need to avoid failure. To move forward, I had to look back. Remembering the experience of failing to get into law school, I realized I had to find a way to take a risk and step off the traditional success ladder.

Eventually, my husband and I agreed that I would take some time out and pursue my goal of expanding into something that empowered me to apply my experience in teaching and counseling to bigger-picture issues. It was a hard call to make because it meant that I wouldn't be contributing to the family finances in the way I had been. As a strong, independent woman dedicated to contributing at least as much as I had before, this felt like a step backward. I began to look deeper than my paper qual-ifications and the conventional leadership equations. I embraced my strengths and their connection to my ambition so that I could release myself from the traditional boundaries and the hierarchy of school-based titles and be open to new possibilities of how I defined leadership and success. It was terrifying and completely contrary to what I thought I was supposed to do, but in the end, it bought me time and energy to refocus. Eventually, I took a position with a consulting firm in the United States. As Robert Frost would say, that has made all the difference.

Aleasha talked about being guided by conventional wisdom. Success and failure are both social constructs, and their interpretations can prove to be immensely rewarding or wholly limiting. Aleasha realized she needed to establish her own definitions to move forward.

In the midst of this messy life pivot, it hit me just how much I found myself reflected in so many of the women leaders I had met. While they appeared confident on the surface, asking only a few questions let me see what lay underneath: we were con-flicted, confused, isolated, and paralyzed by the paradox of being afraid to succeed. Clearly, there was work to be done here. So, I created a leadership development coach-ing practice that is not just about discrete skill advancement. It is first and foremost about helping leaders to gain a deep understanding of their strengths, to know their purpose, to be aware of faulty thinking, and to create a pathway to leadership that works for them—even if that means creating a title that doesn't exist yet. Women leaders often find that they no longer recognize themselves. They have strayed far from their strengths, set aside their needs, and lost focus on the reason they got into lead-ership in the first place. I have heard this story over and over again. And I recognize it because it is my leadership story, too. As soon as I was able to let go of the need to climb a ladder that isn't necessarily welcoming toward women, I freed myself to fly higher, grow strong, and help women who find themselves on the same path.

Aleasha's story highlights the power of redefining success, taking risks, and thinking outside the box. Too often, we are constrained by how others define success, and when our own experiences do not align with that, it can lead to self-doubt. When Aleasha realized that a direct path into educational leadership would not fulfill her in the way that counseling did, she understood that she needed to redefine what she wanted for her life. Breaking out of that predefined idea of success took courage and a tremendous leap of faith. But once Aleasha allowed herself to change directions, she moved quickly along her new path. Finding the courage to trust herself ushered Aleasha into deeply fulfilling work to support other women leaders. In this chapter, you'll look closely at the lessons Aleasha learned and reflect on how these qualities inform your experiences as a leader.

Leadership Lessons

Aleasha recognized that her journey to become an educational leader was going to look a little different from the traditional path to leadership. She found fulfillment in supporting educators in their journeys, working side-by-side with women leaders as they reconnected with their purpose and began to focus on their strengths. Embracing her instincts, rather than sticking to the safe path women are so often conditioned to follow, utterly transformed Aleasha's career. Let's examine the core strategies that worked for her.

Redefining Success

Aleasha's childhood taught her to push forward, work hard, and do well. In adulthood, however, she realized that there was very little joy in the traditional path she had taken. She wanted a different version of success than that formula had to offer. She knew she had to be honest with herself about her needs, her strengths, and her potential.

Many women have realized traditional definitions of success—such as money and power—don't align with their vision of success. They're unwilling to buy into a narrative that requires them to push themselves toward burnout. They prioritize well-being, wisdom, wonder, and mentorship. Leaders need to protect their own human capital, which includes empathy, compassion, and willingness to give back.

REFLECTION QUESTIONS

Reflect on the following questions.

○ What would you say are your strengths? What would others say are your strengths?

○ What barriers do you face to success?

○ What does your personal vision of success look like?

If you are feeling stuck, like Aleasha and so many other women do when striving for an externally defined version of success, how might you reframe that goal to reach it? Figure 5.1 asks you to reflect on what you want to achieve, determine how you'll know when you have succeeded, consider barriers to achievement, and then consider redefining your vision of success.

Taking Risks

Failure was not an option for Aleasha. Success was the only choice, which meant that for many years she took the steps she thought would lead her to success. Traditional routes to success involve obtaining titles in a specific sequence, and climbing the ladder. Women are bound to the ladder if they wish to achieve, and yet, the ladder tends to favor men over women.

A primary reason for this is that the simple definition of success has been largely tied to traditional expectations of males. In a forty-year study of gifted men and women, researchers found that while men and women may perceive themselves as equally successful, their metric for measuring success was different (Lubinski, Benbow, & Kell, 2014). Men defined success as the extent to which they were able to make tangible contributions to the household, while women gauged success by the energy and commitment they made to their households, even if their income was lower than that of their spouse.

Aleasha's commitment to success at all costs was based on a predominantly male definition of success. As a result, she was unwilling to take risks in the direction of what motivated and fulfilled her. It wasn't until she realized that her success could look different that she was able to step off the ladder altogether.

REFLECTION QUESTIONS
Reflect on the following questions.

○ Recall in detail a time in your life when you took a risk that turned out well. What propelled you to take action, in spite of the risk?

○ Removing external factors like luck, right timing, and support of others, what is it about your actions or attitudes that made that risk worthwhile?

○ To what extent has your success been defined by parameters that were not suited to your path? How might you be able to adjust those parameters to have a more reliable measure of success?

Question 1: What is something you want to achieve? Write down one of your goals.	
Question 2: How will you know you have succeeded?	
Question 3: What barriers do you face because of your current definition of success?	
Question 4: How else might you know you have succeeded? In other words, rethink how you could measure success.	
Exercise: Based on your answer to Question 4, creatively rephrase your goal to reflect your newly defined measure of success.	

FIGURE 5.1: Worksheet for teasing out creative thinking around success.
Visit **go.SolutionTree.com/leadership** *for a free reproducible version of this figure.*

Thinking Outside the Box

Aleasha saw firsthand how, in her life and the lives of the women she coached, perfectionism played a massive role in making or breaking women's paths forward. Where perfectionism was tied to an externally imposed understanding of success, wanting to get everything right was not a help but a hindrance.

In *Invisible Women: Data Bias in a World Designed for Men*, author, journalist, and activist Caroline Criado Perez (2019) writes that research over the years on almost all areas of society has taken a "male-unless-otherwise-indicated approach" (p. 3). The implication is that generalized knowledge is almost always skewed in the favor of men—from language use to public restroom design to airplane cockpit measurements, the world has largely been constructed for men. It stands to reason then that the definition of success has favored men as well. As a result, women leaders must think outside of those traditional constructs to find the type of leadership that is the right fit for them.

REFLECTION QUESTIONS

Reflect on the following questions.

○ Has your career followed a straight path to success? Or, like Aleasha, have you followed a winding path, choosing to let go of the need for things to go perfectly according to plan?

○ How has out-of-the-box thinking been important to your work as a leader?

○ In what ways do you feel you still need to stretch yourself to think and act outside of traditional constructs?

Food for Thought

Researcher and author Brené Brown (2012) defines *vulnerability* as "uncertainty, risk, and emotional exposure" (p. 34). In *Daring Greatly*, she urges readers to put aside the traditional interpretation of vulnerability as bad, negative, or weak and to reframe it as the very fountain of joy, fulfillment, and success. Brown (2012) states, "It starts to make sense that we dismiss vulnerability as weakness only when we realize that we've confused *feeling* with *failing* and *emotions* with *liabilities*" (p. 34). Remember that success is a social construct that has been defined by a society that, for hundreds of years, has depended on a male-dominated vision of success where strength and power have prevailed. For women to be successful, they must either adapt to a traditional model that is rarely aligned with typically female strengths or redefine what success actually looks like, a model that allows for vulnerability and holds a space for emotions. As Brown (2012) says:

> If we want to reclaim the essential emotional part of our lives and reignite our passion and purpose, we have to learn how to own and engage with our vulnerability and how to feel the emotions that come with it. . . . And yes, we're taking a huge emotional risk when we allow ourselves to be vulnerable. But there's no equation where taking risks, braving uncertainty, and opening ourselves up to emotional exposure equals weakness. (pp. 35, 37)

Women leaders exhibit incredible strength when they challenge traditions that have historically been limiting or confining. For women, challenging male-dominated notions of success takes great courage because it requires us to write our stories as we go, rather than relying on a predefined mold.

Conclusion

Aleasha's story highlights how a leader can redefine success, take risks, and think outside the box. Accomplishing these goals requires women to develop their muscles for self-awareness, a running theme throughout *Raise Her Up*. Self-awareness is important because when we have a better understanding of ourselves, we can experience ourselves as unique and separate individuals with a unique path to fulfillment. We are then empowered to make changes and to build on our strengths as well as identify areas where we would like to make improvements.

As we mentioned in chapter 4 (page 53), believing in yourself is the first step to success. Aleasha did this again and again throughout her career. She showed up for herself. She grew through the process—not because of a particular outcome—and became more resilient and confident. When women align themselves with their inner knowing, which often does lead them to color outside the lines, they learn to be adaptable. By stepping off the single track given to them by society, they open to new and creative solutions tailored to their unique strengths and circumstances. What seems like a huge gamble actually turns out to be the key to navigating an ever-evolving world.

ALEASHA'S LEADERSHIP LESSONS
Redefining success
Taking risks
Thinking outside the box

References and Resources

Brown, B. (2012). *Daring greatly: How the courage to be vulnerable transforms the way we live, love, parent, and lead.* New York: Penguin.

Carter, N. M., & Silva, C. (2011). *Report: The myth of the ideal worker—Does doing all the right things really get women ahead?* Accessed at www.catalyst.org/research /the-myth-of-the-ideal-worker-does-doing-all-the-right-things-really-get-women -ahead/ on July 19, 2021.

Hauser, F. (2019). *The myth of the nice girl: Achieving a career you love without becoming a person you hate.* Boston: Houghton Mifflin Harcourt.

Hunt, J. (2020). *Unlocking your authentic self: Overcoming imposter syndrome, enhancing self-confidence, and banishing self-doubt.* Little Rock, AR: Author.

Lubinski, D., Benbow, C. P., & Kell, H. J. (2014). Life paths and accomplishments of mathematically precocious males and females four decades later. *Psychology Science, 25*(12), 2217–2232.

Perez, C. C. (2019). *Invisible women: Data bias in a world designed for men.* New York: Abrams Press.

Sukel, K. (2016). *The art of risk: The new science of courage, caution and chance.* Washington, DC: National Geographic Society.

Young, V. (2011). *The secret thoughts of successful women: Why capable people suffer from the impostor syndrome and how to thrive in spite of it.* New York: Three Rivers Press.

CHAPTER 6

On Building Relationships and Blazing Trails

*Change happens by listening and then
starting a dialogue with the people who are doing
something you don't believe is right.*

—JANE GOODALL

PAULINE'S STORY
PAULINE O'BRIEN

The thread that runs through my life is my access to strong women, each of whom came from different walks of life and with varied backgrounds. But they all shared one thing in common: they were resilient. It is so important to know your core strengths. It took me years into my adult working life to understand I had them. I thought everyone was strong, resilient, organized, and compassionate.

Being brought up in a large Irish family full of strong females, I didn't think about core strengths. My family certainly didn't talk about them. We soaked up our environment like sponges; we learned team dynamics, negotiation skills, and strategic thinking without really being aware. My mum was a feisty, capable woman. She was a role model, and she instilled a strong work ethic in me. My dad was not a healthy man, so it was up to my mother to provide for our family, which she did in many inventive ways. She was never out of work and always had something up her sleeve to generate an income. One of her ventures was an egg business. I supported her by helping out after school. She would pick me up, and together, we went selling eggs door to door. My mum taught me to record the tips I received in a notebook. I learned about profit margins, sales, and customer service—and all the time my mum made it seem like a big game.

I enjoyed national schooling in Ireland, but I wouldn't say that people were busy with my future in a planned and encouraging way. Most teachers were focused on getting us through the syllabus and the content. We weren't allowed to dream; we had to pass the exams. Three female teachers were the exceptions. They recognized I was bright, intuitive, and interested—and they invested in me. They provided me with the ability to sketch out what my future could look like. In primary school, I was chosen by my entire school as Best Girl of the School for my leadership, kindness, thoughtfulness, and sense of fun. Because these teachers cultivated a relationship with me and encouraged me to ask questions, I felt I was safe to be myself. I was twelve years old at that time and had no idea the impact of such an award. My parents were very proud but did not share this overtly with me. I've since learned that children need recognition of and open celebration for their achievements. Nevertheless, it was a transformative moment in my life; it gave me confidence to follow my pathway. The lesson I've taken from this is to talk to my daughters, ensuring that they know what their core strengths are, they know their value, and they recognize what they are good at and what they need to work on. They are able to articulate their strengths in a way that I never could.

Knowing her strengths emerged for Pauline as a critical element of her development into adulthood. It was only later in life, for instance, that she realized that everything she had learned as a child helping her mother had become foundational in adulthood: possessing a strong work ethic, running a business, emphasizing customer service, and shaping relationships with clients. Her mom made gaining the trust of other families to buy eggs from Pauline a game, but for Pauline, these were building blocks for her future. In adulthood, and in parenthood, Pauline learned the value of giving voice to strengths.

At the age of seventeen, high school diploma in hand, I deferred my university place for a gap year. I wanted to travel. For years, I had watched planes fly overhead, and I always thought, One day I'll be in one of those planes. *Little did I know that international travel would come to define not only my career but my recognition that how children form friendships and nurture relationships becomes the basis for future connections and networking. I headed to the Netherlands for an amazing one-year adventure as an au pair. Apart from the family, I knew no one. Within ten days, I had formed a group of friends, all au pairs who were at the schoolyard each day. The group was international, comprising members from across the globe. I knew how to network, and it showed. I formed activity groups, and we became each other's family away from home. These friendships have lasted until today and are truly diverse and inclusive, and those formative relationships didn't stop with my friends.*

My boss—a woman—saw potential in me and became a mentor to me. Even though I was the au pair, she invited me to join distinguished dinners she held for diplomats and foreign dignitaries. I was not "the help"; I was worthy of sitting at the table to learn from and converse with guests. I learned about good food and wine, and about the diplomatic community and their roles. It was fascinating and a wonderful opportunity for a young girl. Following my gap year, my circumstances changed such that I couldn't take up my place in university back in Ireland. I no longer qualified for a grant, and it was out of the question for my parents to take on loans to pay for my education. But I would not be held back. I stayed in the Netherlands, secured a job in an international organization, and went to college at night for six years.

Following my courses in a foreign language was tough yet rewarding, as I was building my skill set. My strong work ethic brought with it many opportunities that I knew how to grab with both hands and run with. Another female mentor in my life pushed me to get out of my comfort zone and develop my leadership skills. I was given tasks to lead and people to manage. I am curious and have always been interested in people. I warm to them, and they tend to tell me their stories. I believe it's my ability to value people that has allowed me to enjoy teamwork over the years. People matter to me, and they know it. I began traveling around the globe on behalf of the organization, working in many countries with people of many different nationalities. I rapidly built intercultural competence—though I didn't recognize that's what was happening, I was just adapting and applying the skills and competencies I had learned throughout my life from strong women. I felt capable, and I was thriving.

By taking advantage of the opportunities before her, Pauline grew quickly into her professional life and she never looked back. She got married young, at twenty-three, and had her first child at thirty. She wanted to build a career and had role models who encouraged her to do so. In 2000, she decided to change jobs. This would give her a welcome break from traveling, especially in light of having a baby at home.

I went to sign up with a recruitment agency, and they offered me a job to open a new branch office. All my skills came to the fore in the new position, as with a laptop and a few leads, I began building a client base, and the Amsterdam office became the international hub of the organization. I worked with large corporations like Shell, ABN Mellon, Nike, Adidas, Diageo, and WebEx, to name a few. I was confident in building relationships, selling by believing in the service I could provide. I juggled my full-time workload with parenting, which was frowned upon at times by my female peers. In 2000, it was still common for Dutch women to give up their careers after childbirth.

In my social groups of mothers, I was the exception. It was not easy. I was often criticized by women for not being a committed mother. It was tough to juggle it all, but I could, and I did.

Over time, I convinced the owner of my organization to allow women with young children to work flexible hours. She agreed, and it became the norm within the organization. I worked hard on talent programs to develop team members from within and to promote internally. We trained women into leadership positions and encouraged them to take the leap. I reached director status in 2012.

The following year was a turning point for me, as my daughters became Dutch champion hip-hop dancers. A Dutch charity asked them to go to Uganda to raise money for kids to go to school. I realized that my children's talent had the ability to make a difference in the lives of others, and I also wanted to work for a group that had a bigger impact. Following the trip to Uganda, early in 2014, I accepted a job with the Council of International Schools (CIS), whose mission and vision were closely aligned with my goals.

I developed the Women in Leadership programs at CIS to encourage female educators to take a leap to leadership roles in schools. Women leaders are underrepresented at the top, and a pay gap still exists. I developed plans to help women articulate their skills and competencies and build their confidence in negotiating for equal packages.

It is easy to follow a trail, a lot harder to blaze one. Pauline blazed a trail in finding a voice for women in the international school sector. She knew that a leader's secret to charting a new course is to use one's position in a strategic way.

It wasn't always easy. But with each fall, I stood up stronger, tried not to make the same mistakes more than twice, and continued to be resilient and hardworking. I grew a thick skin against those who didn't lift me up but tried to hold me back. Of course, I felt wounded at times but never broken. Many women have helped me; others have held me back. It is increasingly important that society teach women to inspire each other, to lift one another up, to carry each other's loads sometimes. I am proud of how women are achieving great things, but we can do more, and we will.

In this chapter, we'll look closely at the lessons Pauline learned on her journey to educational leadership. Pauline's experience speaks to the power of blazing trails, developing cultural awareness, building relationships, and acting with integrity. Despite the setbacks she experienced, Pauline knew that if she kept going and surrounded herself with her loudest supporters, she would continue to rise and support other women to do the same. As you read the lessons and questions in the following paragraphs, reflect on how these qualities inform your experiences as a leader.

Leadership Lessons

As women, we can become extremely busy raising our families, juggling a career, and trying to take care of ourselves. A survey by the Pew Research Center (2013) found that "mothers were much more likely than fathers to report experiencing significant career interruptions in order to attend to their families' needs." In part, they attributed this to the fact that gender roles haven't kept pace with labor force trends. Let's consider the characteristics that allowed Pauline to recognize how women have helped her along her career journey with grace and aplomb.

Blazing Trails

Pauline kept all opportunities open at the forefront of her actions. This gave her the confidence she needed to embrace the cultural changes she encountered as she transitioned from growing up in rural Ireland to working in a robust city in the Netherlands and speaking Dutch. Pauline reinvented herself throughout her career and demonstrated her willingness to take creative pathways.

What gives a trailblazer the dedication, passion, and vision they need to brave the unknown? Recent research credits pioneers with a unique level of neuroplasticity, a trait AETHOS Consulting Group CEO Keith Kefgen (2018) calls the *wild brain*. Kefgen (2018) describes the results of his study of trailblazers:

> *Something remarkable happens in the minds of trailblazing leaders, which parallels near "superhuman" flexibility and proficiency in their cognitive abilities. . . . Whereas normal brains filter information to maintain a functional segregation among perceptions, thoughts and feelings, the brains of superior leaders with frequent so-called flashes of genius or entrepreneurial intuition instead seem to show more unfiltered cross-talk among different brain regions. The result is a "wild brain" with the raw capacity to perceive and process external and internal information beyond the capabilities of average people.*

Having a wild brain does come with challenges, though. Kefgen (2018) recommends four practices for trailblazers to keep in mind.

1. **Prioritize understanding:** Colleagues won't always understand the abstract and intuitive ways a leader's wild brain works. Be patient, encourage people to ask questions, and thoroughly explain your rationale.

2. **Set realistic performance expectations:** The wild brain sets a grueling pace that others struggle to match. Set expectations based on what your teammates can do rather than setting the bar by your work ethic or mental capacity.

3. **Recognize and manage stressors:** The wild brain is susceptible to chronic stressors like moodiness and depression sometimes manifesting as extremism or impulsivity. Notice when and how you're prone to such tendencies and find healthy outlets to cope with these stressors.

4. **Find a coach, mentor, or board of advisors:** Trailblazers benefit from meeting with a coach, mentor, or team of advisors. Seek the support of others, knowing that it's a sign of maturity and strength rather than weakness.

To what extent have you blazed trails, big or small? Using figure 6.1, reflect on situations in which you acted as a trailblazer, and identify what you did to demonstrate that quality. Write about actions you took, words or phrases you used to communicate, and the emotions or feelings that came up during the experience.

REFLECTION QUESTIONS

Reflect on the following questions.

- o What does it mean for women in leadership positions to be trailblazers?

- o How does acting as a trailblazer open avenues for others to follow in your footsteps?

- o Which of Kefgen's (2018) recommendations would be helpful to implement in your work?

Developing Cultural Awareness

Cultural context is critical, especially in an international setting. Pauline didn't allow language to become a barrier to communication; she found ways to convey the most essential ideas to her colleagues and among teammates. She quickly identified what mattered in the lives of the people around her. As an international recruiter, Pauline learned to adapt to many different cultural situations as she traveled around the world with her work.

Leaders must model inclusivity. In increasingly diverse teams and workplaces, leaders and their colleagues benefit from becoming more at ease with cross-cultural sensitivity. How can they do this? By becoming aware of their cultural identities and those of their colleagues. By becoming conscious of cultural biases, practicing self-awareness, and striving to be an active listener. Leaders must commit to developing cultural fluency and appreciating the dynamics of their teams.

Identify a situation in which you acted as a trailblazer.	
What actions did you take?	
What emotions or feelings did you experience?	
How did the experience open new avenues for others to follow in your footsteps?	

FIGURE 6.1: Worksheet for teasing out trailblazing attributes.
*Visit **go.SolutionTree.com/leadership** for a free reproducible version of this figure.*

REFLECTION QUESTIONS

Reflect on the following questions.

○ What does it mean to be culturally aware?

○ When has cultural competence been essential to your life and work?

○ What practical steps can you take to celebrate the diverse identities represented in your team?

Building Relationships

Looking after children, meeting other au pairs who were experiencing similar life changes, and being open to learning a new culture were just some of the ways that Pauline built relationships in her growing community. Her commitment to the people she led gave them the confidence to take risks, raising the bar on their own professional expectations.

Powerful leaders develop a positive relationship with their staff. A successful leadership relationship inspires people to become more than they imagined, and helps them achieve more than they ever thought they could. Executive leadership coach Darin Rowell (2019) recommends that leaders consider three traits as they build transformational relationships with their colleagues.

1. **A clear purpose:** Strong leaders set the tone for the relationship. Failing to set intentional expectations leaves room for uncertainty. Establish a clear and intentional basis for the relationship.

2. **An understanding of the type of relationship needed:** Relationships exist along a spectrum. Transactional relationships, such as one you would share with a salesperson, require very little input or responsibility. However, a transformational relationship requires trust, vulnerability, and mutual care. Recognize where your relationships with colleagues fall along the spectrum, and commit the necessary resources to nurture them.

3. **A commitment to pursuing the relationship even when times get tough:** Creating meaningful relationships is a process that emerges over time. Transformational relationships in particular require each person to commit to addressing conflict, repairing any ruptures that occur, and navigating disagreements. Invest in building the competencies needed to maintain powerful professional relationships for the long haul.

Think about the relationships you're building with colleagues. Do they reflect Rowell's (2019) three traits? When your colleagues trust you, they are invested in building a successful organization.

- What have you learned by observing your colleagues and boss in meetings or other work interactions?

- Which of Rowell's (2019) three traits resonated with you most? How do you see these traits at work in your professional relationships?

- How do you build trust in your position? How do your colleagues build trust in you?

Acting With Integrity

Pauline placed the well-being of her constituents—the women applying for leadership positions in the international community—at the forefront of all her decisions. She stood for trust, safety, and justice, and in doing so, she modeled for the rest of the community the kind of behavior she would expect of others. Sitting on various boards, Pauline advocates for women leaders in the entire international school sector, a space that historically has been dominated by White men.

Educational leaders face all kinds of challenges, which require an ability to act with integrity. When you know who you are and what you value, it's much easier to determine your course of action instead of falling prey to indecision or acting to appease others. Professor and frequent contributor to *Harvard Business Review* Clayton Christensen (2011) writes, "It's easier to hold to your principles 100% of the time than it is to hold to them 98% of the time. . . . You've got to define for yourself what you stand for and draw the line" (p. 11). In both her personal life and her career, Pauline never doubted what she stood for. She consistently acted in alignment with her values.

- Do you agree with Christensen's statement? Why or why not?

- When have you been tested, and what strategies did you use to hold tight to your beliefs?

- What aspects of your work challenge you to act with integrity, and how do you rely on your values to support you?

Food for Thought

In an article for *Harvard Business Review*, authors Jack Zenger and Joseph Folkman (2019) discuss the discrepancy between the way women perceive weaknesses in their leadership skills and the reality of how their peers perceive them. Their research shows that women outrank men in significant leadership qualities, such as taking initiative, resilience, bold leadership, building relationships, and championing change.

This is a theme that emerges throughout *Raise Her Up*: celebrating the unique and sometimes surprising qualities that enable women to thrive in leadership roles. Focusing on people first was one of Pauline's most powerful traits, allowing her to build trust and create long-term relationships with schools and communities.

Conclusion

Trailblazers, whatever their age or whichever generation they belong to, are the ones who renew the rules of engagement. They set their own internal compass to their true north. Being the first to chart a new course is not enough; a trailblazer leaves a path that others want to follow. Throughout her professional life, Pauline raised this level of trailblazing to an art form. She has been passionate about investing her skills and creative energy into building things that will have real and lasting value—businesses, family, causes, relationships, and reputations. She was a trailblazer in so many parts of her life, whether it was selling eggs from her family farm to conducting searches for women leaders in international schools. Trailblazers build new paths: they are not afraid to push the envelope and take risks.

PAULINE'S LEADERSHIP LESSONS

Blazing trails

Developing cultural awareness

Building relationships

Acting with integrity

References and Resources

Christensen, C. M. (2011). How will you measure your life? In *HBR's 10 must reads on managing yourself* (p. 11). Boston: Harvard Business Review Press.

Kefgen, K. (2018, June 4). Inside the wild brains of trailblazing leaders. *Forbes.* Accessed at www.forbes.com/sites/forbeshumanresourcescouncil/2018/06/04/inside-the-wild-brains-of-trailblazing-leaders/?sh=66bc37876a55 on December 6, 2021.

Parker, K. (2015, October 1). *Women more than men adjust their careers for family life*. Accessed at www.pewresearch.org/fact-tank/2015/10/01/women-more-than-men-adjust-their-careers-for-family-life/ on July 19, 2021.

Pew Research Center. (2013, December 11). *On pay gap, millennial women near parity—for now*. Accessed at www.pewresearch.org/social-trends/2013/12/11/on-pay-gap-millennial-women-near-parity-for-now/#the-balancing-act on July 15, 2021.

Porritt, V., & Featherstone, K. (Eds.). (2019). *10% braver: Inspiring women to lead education*. London: SAGE.

Rowell, D. (2019, August 8). 3 traits of a strong professional relationship. *Harvard Business Review*. Accessed at https://hbr.org/2019/08/3-traits-of-a-strong-professional-relationship on December 7, 2021.

Zenger, J., & Folkman, J. (2019, June 25). Research: Women score higher than men in most leadership skills. *Harvard Business Review*. Accessed at https://hbr.org/2019/06/research-women-score-higher-than-men-in-most-leadership-skills on July 19, 2021.

CHAPTER 7

On Learning Self-Care

*We think, mistakenly, that success is the
result of the amount of time we put in at work,
instead of the quality of time we put in.*

—ARIANNA HUFFINGTON

FRANCESCA'S STORY
FRANCESCA MULAZZI

*From an early age, I was surrounded by powerful women who inspired me to be
smart and to ask questions. As a young teenager, I spent hours babysitting the neighborhood kids, and looking back, I see how two neighbors nurtured me just as much as
I took care of their children. Dr. Sue invited me to spend many afternoons after school
with her when I struggled to connect with friends my own age. Caroline, another
next-door neighbor, was an independent-minded, progressive therapist who questioned everything happening in our small town and modeled how to challenge norms.
I was a confused teenager struggling to fit in, and both Sue and Caroline treated
me like an adult. They encouraged me to be myself and be patient until I could
find "my people." I was far from being the smartest student in the school, but I was
inquisitive and asked a lot of questions, regardless of how my peers perceived them.
My social studies teacher recognized this need in me to learn more and awarded me
the Phenomenal Woman Award. Between the supportive neighborhood women and
my social studies teacher, I learned that being actively engaged in the world around
me was a good thing, and I was taught that my voice belonged.*

*Fast forward through graduating high school, attending the University of Vermont,
teaching at the Rabat American School in Morocco, obtaining a master's in educational leadership from the University of Oregon, and four years of teaching English
language acquisition at a bilingual public school in Providence, Rhode Island.*

I eventually landed in China, at the Shanghai American School (SAS), where I taught English learners. Five years at SAS taught me the foundational skills for everything else I have done in my professional career, including advocating for students who need support and encouragement. A combination of mentors and professional learning opportunities led me to enroll in the Certificate of Advanced Graduate Studies program with Plymouth State University. Plymouth State had partnered with SAS to support professional learning for their teachers, and although I hadn't yet determined whether this would be my future, this certificate gave me the credentials just in case: not only would I receive leadership training, but I would also obtain a New Hampshire principal certification.

Soon thereafter, the high school principal at the SAS saw leadership potential in me even before I did, and he encouraged me to apply for one of two middle school vice principal positions opening that year. I was the only woman to make it to the finalist round from a pool of more than eighteen applicants, but I didn't get the job. One of the search committee members shared feedback: "Your energy takes up a lot of space in the room."

Reflecting on the support Francesca received as a teenager from strong role models who believed in the power of voice and the importance of asking questions, it is clear that she was in many ways given permission to use her voice. She was encouraged to develop her curiosity and to ask the hard questions. As a professional, this translated into a need to assertively and loudly advocate for student learning. Francesca, who walked into adulthood understanding the value of her voice, believed that this was her mission. And yet, when she applied for the middle school vice principal position, she received feedback that suggested instead that her voice was too loud, that she dominated the room, and not necessarily in a good way. With this tremendous blow to her confidence, Francesca had to step back and rethink her approach.

I channeled my anger and disappointment into hunger for the next opportunity and was determined to learn as much as I could as I embarked on the last step in my principal training: the practicum. I created projects with five different leaders at the school (the superintendent, deputy superintendent, and elementary, middle, and high school principals) and was invited to observe and engage in the many aspects of school leadership.

It was during the practicum that I became deeply engaged in the process of watching leadership as it happened. My work with the principals gave me the opportunity to experience mentorship at its best, and I learned what it meant to lead with equanimity. The lower school principal invited me to observe conversations with her elementary school's Faculty Advisory Team, a solution-oriented group that identified problems and presented solutions, and in our weekly debriefing sessions after those conversations, she would reflect and share her own questions about the meetings. I felt honored by the depth of her trust in me. I learned the importance of being invited to the table and that information comes with trust.

I also had the good fortune to observe the two middle school leaders who exuded calm and radiated kindness every single day. Under their leadership, we initiated and developed a 1:1 laptop program, began standards-based learning, and improved teaching and learning for English as an Additional Language (EAL) students at breakneck speeds. I never saw either one of them get mad, angry, or unprofessional. They asked thoughtful questions. They listened deeply. In the maelstrom of business that SAS embodied, I didn't understand how they could lead the middle school division with such tranquility and consistent compassion for others. That calm radiated through everything they did, even in the most hectic times. I started to ask myself, How do I learn to be more like them? How can I remain focused and manage my energy in this way? How could these people be such powerful leaders without spilling energy that takes up "so much space in the room"?

Francesca completed her Principal's Certification and, with the knowledge that she was genuinely ready for the next challenge after five years in Shanghai, she began the search for her next international position. She had become close with the former deputy superintendent at SAS who had since become director of the International School of Aruba. Having witnessed Francesca's growth during her time at SAS, the director reached out to Francesca to offer her a leadership position in Aruba.

No principal training program really prepares you for the actual first months on the job. To describe it as overwhelming is an understatement. The principalship in Aruba was a maelstrom of tasks to do, things to fix, and decisions to make. The job covered the entire school, from the Montessori kindergarten through grade 12. I handled everything from bus logistics, to disciplining first graders who put rocks in the toilet, to managing the Advanced Placement exams, to setting up and proctoring SAT exams, to observing teachers, to leading the mathematics curriculum review team, to supporting the head as she raised money for a new arts building, and translating English into Spanish to assist our admissions officer interviewing Venezuelan families. Oh, and I played the role of de facto counselor to a parent who was in the process of divorcing her husband and provided a shoulder to cry on for a teacher who was experiencing mental health challenges. I was also humbled when a fifteen-year-old student came out to me, the first adult he had told. Variety is the spice of life, quotes that famous saying, but the spectrum of tasks that faced me every day wore me down within a very short time.

Self-doubt flooded my brain. Is this the principalship, I wondered? How do you get ahead of these tasks? How could I organize my day so that I wasn't in constant reaction mode? Am I doing this right? What's wrong with me? Where is that calm that I saw in my mentors at SAS? I worked seven days a week and still didn't complete all the tasks that needed attention. I had no rhythm and no balance of mind. Not only was it physically exhausting to work ten-hour days, but it was emotionally draining as well. I was constantly in motion, and my mind never stopped. I would never be able to sustain this pace without burning out.

I effected positive change and helped the school to grow in many ways; in other ways, I made mistake after mistake. It was my first principalship, and I made all the classic errors. I emailed too much instead of talking to teachers. I made decisions about how to run activities without first asking how they had been done in the past. I made assumptions about what teachers wanted. I didn't gauge the pace that was comfortable for the teachers. And I didn't listen enough. I felt disillusioned and dissatisfied with my work, two key facets of burnout.

A time-out came at just the right time. While Shanghai had been rewarding for both my partner and me, Aruba was not working for him. Compounding the challenges of life overseas is the fact that adapting to culture shock and adjusting to life in a new country happen at different speeds. I loved Aruba; burnout aside, I was working hard and enjoying the learning, while my husband was bored and professionally unchallenged. So, he got a new job in a secluded area of Mozambique, and we moved. We had relocated to Aruba from Shanghai for the opportunities that my job presented. It was my turn to follow him for the opportunity of a lifetime for his career.

Beira, Mozambique, is a port town whose claim to fame is that it provides the closest ocean and port access to landlocked countries in Southern Africa: Zimbabwe, Zambia, Malawi, and the southern Democratic Republic of Congo. It didn't have an international school. It didn't have any job opportunities. But I had free time. So, I did what came naturally to me: I became a student again. First, I became a student of mindfulness meditation. I listened to old Jon Kabat-Zinn recordings and learned to be still. I learned to sit and developed a daily practice that helped me to center myself, to sit with anger and negative feelings, and to breathe deeply. I learned to identify feelings and recognize their manifestation in my body. Some of the stress I'd experienced in Aruba was physical exhaustion and agitation that lived in my chest. In Beira, I transformed my life: I was still, and I read and reflected silently for hours at a stretch. Compared to the work in Aruba that was often three to eleven-minute bursts of action, this sustained focus was nourishing.

I also formally became a student of leadership when I enrolled in the Plymouth State University (PSU) doctoral program for educational and community leadership. I landed in the program with two burning questions: (1) Was my experience as a principal in Aruba the typical experience? and (2) How do principals manage stress and maintain equanimity? I was still stuck on my question of how to develop equanimity. The cohort model in my doctoral program meant that I spent four summers in residence with twenty-five other students in Plymouth, New Hampshire, reading, researching, and making meaning together. It was perfect timing.

Eventually, through a close connection I had made in my doctoral program, I was offered a job in Lusaka, the capital of the neighboring country of Zambia, combining the roles of English teacher, EAL teacher, and differentiation coach. While I was disappointed to not step back into leadership right away, the job at American International School of Lusaka (AISL) was an ideal chance for me to advocate for students. Differentiation coaches advocate for students by working with teachers to develop strategies to challenge the high-flyers and scaffold support for the students with more needs. EAL teachers advocate for students; in my collaboration with content teachers, I constantly stressed the need for them to explicitly teach subject-specific vocabulary and reading comprehension strategies, which secondary school teachers often fail to do.

It was humbling to be back in the classroom after running part of the show in Aruba. I worked harder than ever; I was flexible and adapted to a role in student advocacy that was familiar to me. Reflecting back on it now, I see that the four years I spent in Zambia focused on using my loud voice for student advocacy while developing inner balance. Within two years, I was back in leadership roles, taking the position of International Baccalaureate (IB) Diploma Programme Coordinator, Extended Essay Coordinator, and Creativity, Activity, and Service Coordinator. Within each of these roles, I was advocating for students, tailoring the student experience, engaging with student voices, and empowering students to take ownership of their learning. I was proud that among our forty-five IB diploma program candidates, we had one student score a 44 (success!) while another scored 24 (success!) with her inclusive access arrangements that included a reader, a scribe, extended time, and a separate room for her exams. I facilitated student success across the spectrum of expectations. I was implementing the school's vision that every student can thrive. I was also applying my own new leadership style, listening more, purposefully pausing, and attempting to balance my energy. But through all this work, the burnout I experienced in Aruba hadn't returned. I had learned how to engage in the kinds of self-care that ensured I had sustained capacity to serve myself, those I loved, and my students.

Francesca's story highlights the power of centering one's health and wellness. You have to put your oxygen mask on first before helping others. By keeping your own wellness at the forefront, you are better equipped to support others and to draw boundaries where needed. By committing to reflection, valuing help from others, finding purpose through hardship, and seeking balance, Francesca transformed her experience in leadership. She went from being frazzled and burned out to being grounded, conscious, and intentional. In this chapter, you'll look closely at the lessons Francesca learned and reflect on how these qualities inform your experiences as a leader.

Leadership Lessons

Francesca learned difficult lessons along the way—taking hard hits when applying for leadership positions and giving every ounce of energy she had to her work when she finally was afforded the opportunity to formally lead. She learned to find opportunity in challenge and to grow from the struggles. Let's examine how Francesca's self-care practices supported her personal and professional transformation.

Committing to Reflection

Throughout her life, Francesca asked questions. Thanks to powerful role models in her life, she'd seen firsthand how critical thinking could set a person on a path of personal growth. Her curious nature wasn't always rewarded, though. As a child, she was accused of being too inquisitive, and as an adult, she was told she took up too much space. Even so, she never stopped asking questions; instead, she turned her questions inward and sought to learn from the feedback she was getting. This helped her turn challenge into opportunity, to learn from feedback, and to grow as a professional.

Good leaders are able to reflect on their experiences. Contemporary leadership models place high value on a leader's engagement in active growth and continuous learning (Brand-Boswijk, 2020; Sutton, 2021). Leaders can spend time alone in reflection or work with a coach to learn from their experiences. Regardless of the method they choose, leaders reflect in order to identify different choices they might have made, recognize their strengths, and imagine reproducing successes.

REFLECTION QUESTIONS

Reflect on the following questions.

○ Have you ever been told that a quality you thought was a strength was actually keeping you from progressing? What emotions surfaced? How did you address the experience?

○ If you were talking to a friend through the same experience, what questions would you ask them to help them reflect on and learn from the experience?

○ Reflect on an experience that didn't go as you hoped it would. What went well and what did not go well? How might you reframe your role in the experience to learn from the situation?

Valuing Help From Others

From an early age, Francesca not only recognized that she had a lot to learn from others, but she willingly accepted help. This takes both confidence and humility. It takes tremendous strength to understand that you don't know everything and to commit to learning from others, asking questions and being guided along the way. It was especially important for Francesca along her journey to self-care as she recognized she wanted to learn from the example of the two middle school leaders.

Educators understand that learning happens through collaboration and that teachers come in many different forms. Social learning theory is the idea that we learn best when we are learning with and from others through observation, reflection, and imitation (McLeod, 2016). Psychologist Albert Bandura believed sustained learning happens when children receive the opportunity to first observe a behavior and then practice it (Kurt, 2020).

Medical schools employ this model, dividing the learning process into two main categories: factual (the what) and procedural (the how) (Augustin, 2014). Regardless of what students are learning, it's applying that knowledge that makes learning most meaningful. Once considered the primary way to teach medical techniques, contemporary teaching practices have evolved to include experience, observation, thinking, and action (Kotsis & Chung, 2013). This is best done in the presence of others. If leaders are committed to continual learning and growth, they must be willing to seek and receive feedback from others.

REFLECTION QUESTIONS

Reflect on the following questions.

○ Identify one or two unlikely mentors you've had in your life. What did you want to learn from them and why?

○ What steps did you take to incorporate those lessons into your life?

○ What do you still want to learn? Who can help you do that and how?

Finding Purpose Through Hardship

There is no greater goal in life than finding purpose. However, purpose rarely just appears. It comes from asking questions, seeking answers, trying new things, and often involves a great deal of failure before reaching success. After struggling to find balance, Francesca enrolled in the PSU doctoral program, determined to learn how leaders manage stress and maintain equanimity. Francesca went back to work with newfound purpose born of the hardship she'd experienced and the wisdom she'd gleaned from her classmates.

Veteran teachers and leaders know that their wellness depends on their ability to find purpose in their work despite the hardship inherent in it, just as Francesca learned to do. Author and teacher advocate Tina Boogren (2021) writes that as leaders, we must develop purpose-building wellness routines to help us overcome adversity:

> We wish to avoid the prolonged stress, mental and physical exhaustion, and emotional toll the education profession can take on our overall well-being. And staying close to knowing our why—why we joined this profession—serves our wellness along the way. . . . You understand that your profession will include difficult moments in time—where the costs of this choice for your life's work will outweigh the benefits. And yet, you also know there is no doubt in your mind. Teaching and leading, educating others, is who you are; it is your identity. And knowing this truth is the start of your purpose-building routine. (p. 71)

Francesca grounded her purpose-building routine in mindfulness meditation and solitude. What practices remind you of your purpose through hardship and the difficult moments of your profession?

REFLECTION QUESTIONS

Reflect on the following questions.

○ How would you have defined your purpose when you first started working?

○ How might that purpose have changed in the last ten to fifteen years?

○ If you had to write a mission statement today, what key phrases would you use to articulate your current purpose?

Seeking Balance

Ultimately, Francesca's greatest lesson was about how to be the person she had always been—with greater focus, meaning, and balance. She learned that if she was to be of service to others, she had to prioritize caring for herself. By first looking inward and finding ways to use her voice with balance and equanimity, she became the best advocate she could be for others.

Self-compassion is one of the primary ways we turn inward to care for ourselves. Researchers Lisa Yarnell, Kristin Neff, Oliver Davidson, and Michael Mullarkey (2018) find that women have a tendency to show less self-compassion than men.

Consider the following explanation of self-compassion from *Wisdom and Compassion in Psychotherapy*:

> *Self-compassion entails being warm and understanding toward ourselves when we suffer, fail, or feel inadequate, rather than flagellating ourselves with self-criticism. It recognizes that being imperfect and experiencing life difficulties is inevitable, so we soothe and nurture ourselves when confronting our pain rather than getting angry when life falls short of our ideals. (Neff, 2012, p. 80)*

Leaders must offer self-compassion when they face challenges. They must examine their feelings and shortcomings without judgment, and instead embrace them with kindness and self-love. Seeking inner balance through such practices as self-compassion allows women to lead with grace and self-confidence.

REFLECTION QUESTIONS
Reflect on the following questions.

○ Where do you wish for balance in your professional life?

○ What messages are you sending yourself that might contribute to a lack of balance?

○ What practices can you embrace to engage with self-compassion?

Figure 7.1 (page 92) guides you to think about the balance in your life. Name various elements or tasks to which you devote time and energy. Consider how much energy you currently devote to each area. Assign a percentage to each. What would your ideal percentage be? Where might you want to make some changes? What are some things you could do to move toward a more ideal balance?

Food for Thought

The struggles that stand out in Francesca's story are all too common among women. Research suggests that women have a greater tendency to experience the symptoms of burnout than men (Robinson, 2019; Young, 2018). Not only is it harder for women to acquire leadership positions, but when they do achieve them, they struggle with issues like perfectionism, imposter syndrome, and a need to prove they are worthy of the opportunities.

In her doctoral work, Francesca discovered research that finds principals feel over-loaded, experience overwhelming levels of stress, struggle to manage the challenges of

What elements in your life require your time and energy?	What percentage of your total daily energy do you devote to this element?	What would be your ideal breakdown of energy?	What might you do to help yourself achieve a more ideal balance?
Sample: Family time	**Sample:** 30%	**Sample:** 60%	**Sample:** Work out in the morning while my family is still asleep so I can read with my children in the evening.

FIGURE 7.1: Worksheet for teasing out balance.

*Visit **go.SolutionTree.com/leadership** for a free reproducible version of this figure.*

the role, and encounter emotional exhaustion (Mulazzi, 2018). They also frequently experience "low levels of professional accomplishment, low levels of job satisfaction, and [they conclude that the] countless hours dedicated to the task and responsibilities of the job aren't enough" (Cranston, Ehrich, & Billot, 2003, p. 159). In response, Francesca's work focused on how school administrators can better take on the challenges of the position by focusing on problem-focused engagement strategies and the development of effective coping strategies for dealing with stress. In other words: self-care.

Conclusion

Francesca's story highlights how committing to reflection and valuing others' help support educational leaders to thrive long-term. By intentionally focusing her energy on the things that mattered most, Francesca was able to remain committed even when she faced challenges. Her self-care practices allowed her to expand her capacity, increase her awareness, and target her efforts instead of being frazzled and chaotic.

Reflection allows us to make sense of our experience, to achieve greater understanding of ourselves and the factors that contributed to the experience. It increases our insight and creates pathways to future learning. Francesca also illustrates how critical it is for leaders to recognize the importance of timing. Some matters are urgent, while others require patience. School leaders affect employee morale and a school's success story depending on the decisions they make and when they act on or communicate those decisions. Effective leaders learn how to time their actions depending on the situation. Women leaders are at their best when they commit to cultivating balance, prioritizing personal wellness, and leaning on reflection to illuminate their decision making.

FRANCESCA'S LEADERSHIP LESSONS

Committing to reflection

Valuing help from others

Finding purpose through hardship

Seeking balance

References and Resources

Augustin, M. (2014). How to learn effectively in medical school: Test yourself, learn actively, and repeat in intervals. *Yale Journal of Biology and Medicine, 87*(2), 207–212.

Boogren, T. (2021). *Educator wellness: A guide for sustaining physical, mental, emotional, and social well-being*. Bloomington, IN: Solution Tree Press.

Brand-Boswijk, H. (2020, November 11). *The leader as coach—affecting organisational success and growth from a place of curiosity and empathy*. Accessed at www.thehrdirector.com/features/leadership/leader-coach-affecting-organisational-success-growth-place-curiosity-empathy/ on December 7, 2021.

Center for Contemplative Mind in Society. (n.d.). *The tree of contemplative practices* [Illustration]. Accessed at www.contemplativemind.org/practices/tree on July 19, 2021.

Cranston, N., Ehrich, L., & Billot, J. (2003). The secondary school principalship in Australia and New Zealand: An investigation of changing roles. *Leadership & Policy in Schools, 2*(3), 159.

Kabat-Zinn, J. (2018). *Meditation is not what you think: Mindfulness and why it is so important*. London: Piatkus.

Kotsis, S. V., & Chung, K. C. (2013). Application of the "see one, do one, teach one" concept in surgical training. *Plastic and Reconstructive Surgery, 131*(5), 1194–1201.

Kurt, S. (2020, January 6). *Social learning theory: Albert Bandura*. Accessed at https://educationaltechnology.net/social-learning-theory-albert-bandura/ on February 3, 2022.

McLeod, S. (2016). *Albert Bandura's social learning theory*. Accessed at www.simplypsychology.org/bandura.html on December 7, 2021.

Mulazzi, A. F. (2018). *The relationship between coping skills and burnout in international school principals*. Doctoral dissertation, Plymouth State University, NH.

Neff, K. (2012). The science of self-compassion. In C. Germer & R. Siegel (Eds.), *Wisdom and compassion in psychotherapy* (pp. 79–92). New York: Guilford Press.

Quinn, M. M., & Smith, P. M. (2018). Gender, work, and health. *Annals of Work Exposures and Health, 62*(4), 389–392. Accessed at www.academic.oup.com/annweh/article/62/4/389/4956148 on July 19, 2021.

Robinson, B. (2019, November 6). Women workers are more likely to experience this medical disorder than their male counterparts. *Forbes*. Accessed at www.forbes.com/sites/bryanrobinson/2019/11/06/what-job-illness-do-the-most-accomplished-women-have-in-common on July 19, 2021.

Sutton, J. (2021, November 25). What is the coaching leadership style? *Positive Psychology*. Accessed at https://positivepsychology.com/coaching-leadership-style/?utm_source=rss&utm_medium=rss&utm_campaign=coaching-leadership-style on December 7, 2021.

Yarnell, L. M., Neff, K. D., Davidson, O. A., & Mullarkey, M. (2018). Gender differences in self-compassion: Examining the role of gender role orientation. *Mindfulness, 10*, 1136–1152.

Young, S. (2018, May 31). Women are more likely to suffer work burnout than men, study finds. *The Independent.* Accessed at www.independent.co.uk/life-style /work-burnout-men-women-positions-power-self-esteem-family-balance-study -montreal-a8377096.html on July 19, 2021.

CHAPTER 8

On Valuing Persistence and Trusting Right Timing

Create the highest, grandest vision possible for your life, because you become what you believe.

—OPRAH WINFREY

MAYA'S STORY
MAYA NELSON

I am not sure when my internal voice became loud, but I know it's always been there. As a senior in high school, I remember losing the senior class president election to a boy who may have had height and bravado but not an inkling about the vision, dreams, or plans our class could put into place that year. Upon graduation, I realized I had done all of the organization and planning for the class—all of the championing and dreaming. I was the person behind the scenes who had made things work. That would be the first of many lessons about gender, equity, and leadership. I just didn't realize it at the time. I had no idea that I had a voice or what that voice was trying to tell me, and it wasn't until decades later that I found that voice in the hallways of a school.

Being raised by an Indonesian father and a German mother was my normal, but in the sixties and seventies, bicultural families were not so common. Not only did we have an amalgamation of different traditions and rituals, but we also learned that home was not where we lived as we moved from Tokyo, Japan, to London, England, then on to Hamburg, Germany, and eventually to Jakarta, Indonesia. Given this upbringing, it's no surprise my siblings and I were different from many of the other kids we went to school with. My father believed that it was best to avoid wearing blue jeans, that traveling the world was important, and that understanding language and religions was the key to understanding another person. My mother, staunchly German, believed it was important to have traditions and rituals in the household, that food was not to be wasted, and that family time was critical. Together, my parents modeled that hardships and challenges can be overcome, that you didn't speak about what was hard (which wasn't always good), and that persistence was the key to everything. As an Indonesian Muslim man, my father instilled in his three daughters that education was the ultimate gift, that we could be anything we wanted, and that having conversations about the world and events and learning cultural etiquette and social skills would prepare us for our future. We were a family that didn't necessarily fit into cultural norms or societal expectations. I learned so much from my parents, from the stories they told around the dining room table about their experiences around the world. I also learned from the moments of silence in our home—the uncomfortable moments when we learned about histories not easily shared and the challenges and pain from my parents' past. The dispositions of resilience, stamina, loyalty, and trust came from their histories, their values, their dreams. And, mostly, I learned that you always stand up after you fall.

Because of her Indonesian-German background and her experiences living in multiple countries, Maya felt out of place at university. She struggled to belong, to adjust to social expectations and the distinctive American college culture. This lack of direction lasted until her advisor pulled her aside and encouraged her to set higher expectations for herself.

My advisor was an extraordinary woman who took me under her wing and said, "You can do this. You can learn more than what you are learning from your classes and in the dormitories with your friends and roommates, drinking and partying." So, I listened. I became involved in leadership through running programming for university students. Whether booking athletic activities or famous authors, organizing evening movies, or packing concert halls for thousands, there were aspects of this work—the organization, the coordination, the grit, and even the minor details—that I loved. During the next two years, I became more and more involved in leadership at the university level, running a university organization that not only catered to the 15,000 students on campus but also offered experiences that brought the city community together. On reflection, I realized I learned so much about myself, people, and leadership working those jobs for three years. Ultimately, that was the most meaningful gift my university journey bestowed on me. Though I had my education degrees and had learned the differences between decoding and comprehension, constructivist methods, and developmental approximations of children, the real knowledge I gained was in the face-to-face interactions with my college classmates and my mentor, who took the time to listen and push me out of my comfort zone.

Within a year of graduating college, I was working as a student teacher, learning everything I could about childhood development, special education, elementary education practices, literacy practices and effectiveness, and how to partner with parents. I was desperate to become a full-time teacher and quickly learned that access to the right people would often offer opportunities. So, I learned every secretary's name in the special education department in our district office. I called every day for five weeks. I was persistent. The phone calls became more personal, and soon they knew it was me as soon as they answered the phone. Eventually, this led me to meet the director of pupil services and paved the way for conversations that opened doors. After I'd been calling him for weeks, he relented and said, "I have a project for you!" He asked if I would be willing to start a new program in the district for students who were in hospital wards with significant emotional and behavioral disorders. Never too shy to take on a challenge, and desperate for a job, I said, "Yes!" I realized that sometimes persistence pays off.

Maya could have followed a traditional path—student teaching for a few years, waiting for a full-time teaching position to open up. But she knew early on that she was destined for something bigger and that traditional timelines would not suffice. Maya recognized that while she loved teaching, she also loved the more administrative aspects of education that focused on building programs and running an organization. Her experiences in the inner-city public schools exposed her to both the challenges and joys of education, and she found her purpose—to become an advocate for children. Ultimately, her career took her abroad. During her transition overseas, she realized she was truly in her element.

Moving from the U.S. public school system to the overseas international school system was like coming home for me, the third-culture kid who had seen the world at an early age as my family moved from country to country. I spent seven years teaching overseas in Jakarta and Tokyo and found that living overseas in different countries was really what brought me joy. The unsettled and uncomfortable feeling I'd had in university, as I grappled with where I came from, dissipated. I learned that my comfort was truly found in neighborhoods that felt foreign to me; I loved the feeling of living in cultures that were different from my own, and I thrived when I was exposed to new and unique perspectives.

The qualities I'd learned from my family and in my early career—persistence and trusting in right timing—continued to serve me well as my career progressed.

My teaching career spanned decades as I moved from teaching elementary to special education. Halfway through my career, I moved to Taipei, Taiwan, where I worked at an amazing school: Taipei American School. I started as a teacher for students with learning disabilities, but within a few years I worked on a strategic plan that grew our special education practices. As a result, I became the special education director. In this capacity, I felt like I had found my mojo—it was truly an incredible experience of building a department and, ultimately, a school-within-a-school for students with more moderate learning needs. The head of school was a visionary educator who believed that all students have a place in schools even though inclusive practices were not widely used in international schools. We were a beacon in Asia. Selling the concept and the product of a different program for our community to the board, the parents, the faculty, the students, and the greater Taipei community was all about learning how to create a painting without paint. Special education programs were fairly new to international schools at this time, so designing the program required us to develop new skills to define job descriptions, design learning spaces, plan which students would benefit from the services, and strategize inclusion outcomes. I learned to listen to the stories of parents, students, friends, and even strangers. I learned to listen to children. With listening came trust, and with trust came loyalty. After a year of planning, I had a community of followers who believed in the possibilities. The story became our story and our vision. It was, in one sense, so simple to do; it came from my heart, but it was also difficult because it took time. It was all about establishing people's trust and loyalty. Most importantly, it was about people believing in you enough to take a leap of faith.

Our desire to raise more women leaders was a worthwhile goal, yet getting the job done came with its share of challenges—sometimes more so for women in leadership positions. This was especially evident one day as I came out of a strategic planning meeting. As a Core Planning Committee member, I worked with administrators, educators, and consultants to build the new vision and strategic plan for our school. It was exciting; this was my first opportunity to cultivate a sense of community around shared words and a vision. I sat in the meetings, mesmerized by my teammates' talent and their ability to create and ideate. But I quickly noticed that important words said by women were unnoticed or entirely dismissed. And when men restated women's ideas or words, the accolades would flow. I didn't say anything at that time, but the more involved I became in schoolwide meetings, the more I realized this pattern existed everywhere. When I sat in an action plan meeting with fellow teachers, administrators, board members, and parents, I proposed an idea early on, and no one responded. Toward the end of the meeting, a male administrator repeated my idea, and suddenly everyone thought it was wonderful. This happened not just once but time and again in almost every meeting I attended. Sometimes I tried it just to see what would happen. It was a test. One day as I was walking out of a meeting, a remarkable leader turned to me and said, "Let me give you some advice. Always be the last to speak. Don't throw your idea out first. Someone will take it, and then it's not yours. Wait and learn the body language of those around you, and you will know when things are nearing an end. It works." Her words paved the path of leadership for me in the future. Being the last to talk works remarkably well.

In July 2007, I started a new position as the associate principal at Hong Kong International School. As chance would have it, shortly after I started, the principal announced her decision to leave the following year. These were hectic times—not only was I learning a new job, I was also adjusting to a new lifestyle, raising two young children in a new home, connecting with new people, and adapting to the new school I had just joined. As summer turned to fall, the parent advisory group (a committee of parents who advised the leadership of the division) and head of school approached me about the possibility of interviewing for the principal position. The position had been advertised internationally, and there were three final candidates, including myself. I was the least experienced and likely the most nervous. Five weeks later, I was offered the position. Having watched very competent candidates come and go, I wasn't sure why I was the last one standing, but I felt tremendous excitement and nervousness about the opportunity.

As an educational leader and a woman, I've learned the importance of sharing a sense of belonging and purpose with others. Creating a vision and then building upon that shared picture give people a common path. While we certainly always honor individuality and different perspectives, starting with a shared vision and similar beliefs can sustain the group when times get tough. As a principal in Hong Kong, I had various opportunities to create systemic change and work on large-scale projects. Like in many schools, we changed curriculum practices, added programs, expanded our support systems for students, and hired teachers who would create the learning culture we wanted. We also built our dream early childhood building, a massive undertaking that took six years, countless resources, and many millions of dollars. These experiences required me to examine my beliefs and challenge my thinking about education, our community, and our students' needs.

We faced significant challenges in various projects, and our parent community often responded to change with negativity and discontent. During the difficult times, though, our leadership team and faculty stood together. We believed in our shared vision, and knowing that we had each other's backs was important. What we also learned, though, was that we began to hear in ourselves and each other what we each believed and thought was important. Those truths for us—those values—were what bound our school community together and allowed us to achieve some great accomplishments. I realized that I was in a very public space during that time, and how I handled myself determined the success of our projects and was a reflection on our school. I was able to hold my head high because of the sense of connectivity and community our faculty had.

It has taken me several decades in adulthood to understand myself and know what I want. I recognize that the seeds planted in me long ago have created my personality, disposition, and temperament, all of which allowed me the successes I have had. My courage to question the status quo supports my never-ending quest to do better for others and to champion children in our world. I recognize that each of my positions—each year teaching, each year leading, and each year working with people—has allowed me to grow and supported my quest for the next challenge in life. All of it is personal. And through it all, I have grown.

I have recognized that timing and faith are huge in believing that new opportunities will come. Often, these opportunities don't happen according to your preferred timeline, but they still come in mysterious ways if you allow yourself to be open to them. I also know that the relationships you cultivate, the mentors you have, the friendships that support and nurture you, are instrumental in building your career and growing you as a person and a leader. As leaders, we create other leaders. In going through our respective journeys, we must discard our unconscious bias, support the awakening of others, and create opportunities for those who seek them. And we especially should support these ideals in other women and the children of the world.

In this chapter, we'll look closely at the lessons Maya learned on her journey to becoming a leader and finding her purpose. Maya's experience speaks to the importance of relationships, harnessing your vision, cultivating a shared purpose, and trusting in right timing. Maya knew early on that she was destined to lead, which gave her the courage to follow a non-traditional path. And the wisdom she gained along the way taught her to lead through listening and building trust, to create a sense of belonging and purpose with others. As you read the lessons and questions in the following paragraphs, reflect on how these qualities inform your experiences as a leader.

Leadership Lessons

Maya's move overseas was the game-changer she needed to be able to emerge as a leader. Not only did she find herself in the right places at the right times, but her sense of belonging in international schools allowed her strengths to emerge as she moved in a natural direction toward leadership.

Understanding the Importance of Relationships

Maya intuitively understood that relationships were the key to success, and she developed close, personal connections with the secretaries in the special education department in her district. Ultimately, they would be the gatekeepers who introduced Maya to the director, who offered her a career-changing opportunity. Maya's reliance on close personal connections with people continued throughout her career, and she recognized that her successes were the result of a team effort. Of course, the work Maya did was her own, but each time she was able to create change or implement a new program, that accomplishment was the result of a collaborative effort.

Strong relationships are the foundation for success in any organization because all business depends on meaningful connections between stakeholders (Hovsepian, 2018). School leaders who take the time to get to know their teachers and staff, parents, students, boards, and community members are better able to capitalize on those connections to provide the best possible experience for everyone involved.

REFLECTION QUESTIONS

Reflect on the following questions.

- How do you celebrate your colleagues?
- What practices does your team rely on to complement one another's strengths?
- How do your team's successes reflect the reality that many people are working together to achieve the team's goals?

Harnessing Your Vision

Maya had a vision early on of what she wanted to do and where she wanted to be, and she dedicated herself to that path. When she encountered setbacks and challenges, she relied on her vision to guide her toward her goal. The director of pupil services noticed Maya's tenacity and offered her the opportunity to do something significant.

What are some ways leaders harness their vision to move toward their goals? Some might use a vision board to display images or quotes that represent their aspirations. Others might journal or repeat mantras. Whatever process you use, ultimately, you're tapping into your capacity for visioning. Leaders of THNK School of Creative Leadership Lieselotte Nooyen, Berend-Jan Hilberts, and Menno van Dijk (2014) write that *visioning*, the act of envisioning an outcome, is a powerful ability of successful leaders. "Creative leadership means having such a strong conviction that an idea will work, that its realization is driven with relentless commitment. This compulsive determination is required to push through all the barriers and convince the critics" (Nooyen et al., 2014). If you acknowledge the possibility of change, then change can and will happen.

REFLECTION QUESTIONS

Reflect on the following questions.

- Consider a time when you had a vision for your future. What steps did you take to realize that vision?

- If you were to create a vision board based on one of your goals, what images, quotes, and details would you include?

- What saying or mantra could you create to center you when your vision is challenged?

Tenacity is a primary key to success! Never. Give. Up. When we define what we want in life, we must commit to the actions and habits that move us toward achieving that vision and let go of things that do not. Figure 8.1 asks you to identify your leadership vision and guides you to name the actions, behaviors, and resources that support and hinder you from achieving it.

Cultivating a Shared Purpose

Maya quickly learned that real change was only possible when everyone on her team was working toward shared goals. She learned to use her voice—not only to tell her own story but also to elicit stories from others. In creating a culture of connection around common goals, Maya was able to build trust, buy-in, and loyalty. She understood that success would only be possible through a sense of collective purpose. Meaningful change does not happen overnight. But change that is grounded in common purpose is far more likely to happen, and sooner.

The team at Slack (2021) writes about the importance of developing shared purpose for organizations, especially post-pandemic. When employees feel their work contributes to the greater good, they are more connected and invested: "today's workers want to know that they're working for something deeper than a paycheck" (Slack, 2021). What can leaders do to cultivate shared purpose? Slack (2021) recommends three ways: (1) articulate your organization's purpose, (2) leverage success stories, and (3) eliminate barriers to connection. How might you implement these three elements in your team to cultivate shared purpose? What results might you achieve?

What are the elements of your own leadership vision?	What actions, behaviors, or resources foster that?	What actions, behaviors, or resources hinder it?	What habits or actions can you cultivate to move that vision forward?	What are you willing to let go of to achieve your vision?
Sample: Collaboration	**Sample:** Being a good listener	**Sample:** When I get impatient	**Sample:** Practice compassion.	**Sample:** The need to control the outcome

FIGURE 8.1: Worksheet for teasing out tenacity.

*Visit **go.SolutionTree.com/leadership** for a free reproducible version of this figure.*

REFLECTION QUESTIONS

Reflect on the following questions.

○ What practices allow you to build trust, buy-in, and loyalty within your team or among colleagues?

○ Do you share a sense of collective purpose with your team or colleagues? Why or why not?

○ What practices could you adopt to cultivate shared purpose within your organization?

Trusting in Right Timing

Maya recognized that the timelines she imagined for her life and the timelines that the universe provided didn't always match. But through patience and faith, she realized that when opportunities for growth emerged, the timeline didn't matter. Maya learned to seize the moment, embrace change, and create her own destiny.

Do you know the parable about the person in perilous danger who was convinced that they would be rescued by God? They waited patiently for God to come, turning away frequent offers of help from others because they believed God would save the day. When, after a lifetime of waiting, they meet God at the gates of Heaven, they ask why God didn't come. God responds, "I sent you countless offers of help, but you ignored all the signs." As leaders, we don't always recognize when an opportunity comes our way, but if we stay focused on *possibility*, then we begin to see that we have more control over our lives than we give ourselves credit for. Maybe things look a little different than we expected, but there is hope. Seeing isn't always believing. Sometimes, if you believe, you'll begin to see.

Professors Rose Sherman and Tanya Cohn (2019) suggest that leaders must be willing to trust in right timing in order to make informed decisions: "Leaders can be very excited about new . . . opportunities but know in their gut that the timing might not be right. . . . Leaders need to know when the time is right for their leadership and when it may not be." Sometimes, when we are too focused on a particular path or outcome, it is harder to see the possibility in the unexpected turns our journey might take. By maintaining realistic goals, staying in tune with our inner knowing, and keeping an open mind, we can be ready for new adventures when the time is right.

R EFLECTION Q UESTIONS

Reflect on the following questions.

○ Think of a time when the signs were pointing you to new possibilities, but you didn't recognize them because you felt a need to control the outcome. How might you position yourself in the future so that you'll be open to seeing the possibilities?

○ What tools do you rely on to trust in right timing?

○ What is something you'd like to change so that you're more open to possibility?

Food for Thought

Women leaders see the need for change. They feel compelled to step up. And yet, they're often held back by the voice of their inner critic. In her book *Playing Big: Practical Wisdom for Women Who Want to Speak Up, Create, and Lead*, leadership expert Tara Mohr (2015) suggests women level up by growing their inner mentor. Here are some suggestions she shares.

➤ Ask yourself, "What would my inner mentor do in this situation? What would she say?" Check in with her and see what the answer is.

➤ Make some art about your inner mentor or her home. A collage, drawing, painting, or photographs that evoke her—whatever the medium of choice.

➤ Block off time during the week to spend as she would spend it. For example, take a Sunday evening to spend as she spends her Sunday evening.

➤ Think about what your mentor eats for a meal and prepare that meal yourself.

➤ Choose a day this week to dress like your inner mentor. How does it impact your day?

➤ When you sit to write an email, answer it as though she is answering it. What would you say?

➤ Identify a difficult situation or dilemma in your life and check in internally: How would your inner mentor see it? See how this shifts your perspective.

In an article for *The Sunday Times*, Mohr (2014) tells readers who the inner mentor is and how to connect with her. "The inner mentor is an imagined version of an older, wiser you. . . . Playing big happens when we listen to the voice of the inner mentor," not the inner critic (Mohr, 2014, p. 64). Once you find her, you will realize she exists as a voice within you.

Conclusion

Maya's story illustrates the power of understanding the importance of relationships, harnessing your vision, cultivating a shared purpose, and trusting in right timing. Holding high standards allowed Maya to rise above failure and recognize opportunities to grow. She learned to live in alignment with her inner mentor, crafting an environment that supports a positive and supportive mindset. Leaders must learn to talk to themselves from that higher perspective. If you raise the standards of your mindset as Maya did, you will not be shattered by failures or setbacks. You will participate in healthy competition instead of comparing yourself with others.

MAYA'S LEADERSHIP LESSONS
Understanding the importance of relationships
Harnessing your vision
Cultivating a shared purpose
Trusting in right timing

References and Resources

Carter, N. M., & Silva, C. (2010). *Report: Pipeline's broken promise.* Accessed at www .catalyst.org/research/pipelines-broken-promise/ on July 19, 2021.

Hovsepian, T. (2018, July 20). Business and people: Why relationships are essential for a successful business. *Forbes.* Accessed at www.forbes.com/sites/forbeslacouncil /2018/07/20/business-and-people-why-relationships-are-essential-for-a-successful -business/?sh=639defc974f2 on December 8, 2021.

Klocko, B. A., Justis, R. J., & Kirby, E. A. (2019). Leadership tenacity and public-school superintendents. *Journal of Leadership Education, 18*(1), 1–13.

Mohr, T. (2014, October 5). Live large. *The Sunday Times,* p. 64. Accessed at www .thetimes.co.uk/article/live-large-xjwn2lqtk02 on February 11, 2022.

Mohr, T. (2015). *Playing big: Practice wisdom for women who want to speak up, create, and lead.* New York: Penguin Random House.

Nooyen, L., Hilberts, B.-J., & van Dijk, M. (2014, April 16). *The process of visioning.* Accessed at www.thnk.org/insights/the-process-of-visioning/ on December 8, 2021.

Sherman, R. O., & Cohn, T. M. (2019, October 2). *Leadership challenge: The role of timing in work and life.* Accessed at www.myamericannurse.com/leadership -challenge-the-role-of-timing-in-work-and-life/ on December 8, 2021.

Slack. (2021, September 12). *How shared purpose drives collaboration.* Accessed at https://slack.com/blog/collaboration/shared-purpose-drives-collaboration on December 8, 2021.

CHAPTER 9

On Defying Limits and Leading From the Heart

As women, we have superpowers. We are sisters.
We are healers. We are mothers. We are goddess warriors.

—MERLE DANDRIDGE

SUZETTE'S STORY

SUZETTE JULIEN

We never know where we could end up in life, although each of us has an inner call to do something about the way we feel and think. We may be influenced by someone who gives us an idea, shares a story, or even maps out a journey that becomes a reality. I was born to Caribbean parents who took the quantum leap to seek opportunities in the United States. They, too, did not know how their journey would impact them and their family. My parents believed that education was the way to become a better contributor to society, to have a voice, and to become empowered to help others. They were determined that migrating to the land of plenty would make a difference in education for the family.

I attended public school from elementary through high school. During my final year in high school, I had the opportunity to attend a semester of biology at UMass Boston. I entered college as a nursing student in 1977, and after two years in the program, my nursing advisor, certain that I wouldn't finish, convinced me to change my major. When I realized the timing was not right and the program was not a good fit for me, I enrolled in the teaching college, an institution that would prepare me to challenge students and help them to be confident and proud of who they are. Science had always been one of my favorite subjects, and I excelled and completed my education program. My first teaching assignment, in 1990, was in the Boston

Public Schools system as a science teacher for kindergarten through grade 5. That was an experience that is still vivid in my memory today; it showed me that students learn best by doing. My tenure at the Boston Public Schools was the foundation of a teaching career that spanned several levels in elementary and middle school (remedial reading); it allowed me to craft and hone my skills. I wanted to make a difference for each student, and I saw the twinkle, and eventually the bright light, shining in every student's development.

And still, nursing remained in my subconscious. Knowing that someone felt I could not be a nurse haunted me for years. I felt that part of my life was unfulfilled, and I resented that my dream had been taken away by a single person with little faith in my ability. Determined to prove to myself that I had what it took, I decided to finish my nursing program.

For several years during the late 1980s, I pursued two careers: teaching full time and nursing part time. My nursing job began in the evenings, after teaching all day, and I worked on weekends, holidays, and in the summers. My students were always impressed when I changed into my nursing uniform at the end of the day, knowing I had to race to my nursing job. I loved my work, and I enjoyed working with doctors, and even teaching some new doctors about certain procedures and practices. Most times, my patients did not believe that I, a petite woman of color, was a nurse. Few nurses in my program were women of color, so I stood out.

Suzette was teaching by day and moonlighting as a nurse at night and on the weekends. She loved teaching and learning, yet she wanted to maintain her nurse's license. Over time, however, it became a challenge to manage both careers. She chose to stay in teaching, as she loved being exposed to various cultures and gaining insight into her students' lives.

Being an educator working in the Caribbean has been challenging yet rewarding. My first job began with an invitation to fly overseas to interview for a remedial reading post in a private school whose students were predominantly from middle-class families. I struggled with the demands of the position and the lack of acceptance in the school. I remember being ignored in the staff room until I broke the ice and initiated the conversation. Being an expatriate with Caribbean roots was not the same as being a local. Not to mention I had a strong Bostonian accent. I would often send the students to fetch my pocketbook, and they would return empty-handed claiming there was no book on my desk. I quickly learned to use the word handbag *and other colloquial expressions to make my point, to ensure I was understood and had a voice within the organization.*

After several years teaching remedial reading in local private schools, in 1995, I decided to change jobs to the international school K–12 setting. The international school curriculum was similar to the curriculum I had been exposed to in Boston, so that transition was easier than my work in the local system. I taught for two years at the elementary level before moving into an administration position. The head of school became my mentor, seeing that I was a leader and encouraging me in that direction. I completed my international leadership certification and my master's in international education, and I shadowed women principals in Connecticut. My experience in Connecticut allowed me to gain hands-on experience of how schools are managed. After that experience, I realized I wanted to be a principal, a leader who would encourage and mentor individuals to be leaders to transform their organizations and impact all stakeholders. I understood the importance of mentorship in developing leaders.

Several educational leaders mentored me throughout my career. My experience as a principal was very practical and allowed me to gain confidence in leading teams, developing programs, building relationships with stakeholders, budgeting, problem-solving, and managing an organization. Both women and men mentored me. I have a strong conviction about mentorship, and I have mentored teachers from all levels and disciplines. I mentored many of our local teachers to prepare them for other international teaching positions in India, China, Europe, the United Arab Emirates, and other parts of the Caribbean. Those teachers have written to thank me for the mentorship they received from me and the team. Several of those teachers became leaders in other international schools.

Being a leader in the international setting created a myriad of opportunities for continuous learning. I networked with colleagues around the globe, and I gained insight on how to think differently about cultures. I forged relationships with other colleagues in the field. I have collaborated with an international school in Anguilla that sought to implement the Primary Years Programme. My role was to provide professional development as well as to mentor their principal. My early experiences shaped the leader that I am today, and I wanted to pay it forward and continue learning.

Being mentored had a profound impact on Suzette. Frequently, mentors can spot leadership qualities in others and tap into those skills, building up a potential leader and exposing them to experiences that will enable them to grow. Suzette's mentor asked her to take that leap to administration after her second child was born. Suzette pondered this during maternity leave and decided that, while change is never easy, she'd been presented with an incredible opportunity.

After my maternity leave, I returned ready to take up the position as the first woman of color to be principal of the elementary school (K–6). I was mentored for the position, and although hesitant at first, I knew that I wanted to develop my educational path. I was new to the role, but I was confident that I could work with a team to bring about a change in programs and practices. Any change to the status quo would require research, communication, and unity to move forward. I wanted to help empower women with leadership qualities to be part of our team and learn about change management. I garnered research and championed my philosophy that we are all leaders, and I wanted those who could lead to empower themselves and join the journey in the change process.

The first change in instruction I had to accomplish was to introduce the International Baccalaureate (IB) Primary Years Programme (PYP) in our elementary school. Normally, when schools introduce IB, they begin in the high school; however, I had a vision that could change teaching and learning in the organization. I envisioned a program that would change the face of the classroom and its accountability to students and parents alike, and would encourage students and teachers to be autonomous and guide their learning through inquiry. It would also be a change that required teachers to say no to their comfort zone and eventually change their behavior. As a leader, I believed in the vision of the institution, and I knew that to be a successful leader I would need to work closely with my team to bring the PYP on in order to change instruction.

For two years (2007–2009), the elementary team and I worked feverishly to understand the international program. During that period, teachers received training from International Baccalaureate facilitators and collaborated to better understand the framework. Although we were a candidate school, a few of our board members were unsure about the trajectory, but my team and I were able to convince the board that it was the best practice toward a better teaching and learning environment. By 2009, we were an authorized IB PYP school. Since that time, the program has transformed the school. Teachers speak the same language and collaborate weekly with their grade team teachers and specialist teachers who teach arts, information technology, languages, physical education, and guidance.

The change from traditional education to the PYP created a strong community focused on globalized learning and internationalism. Our students were debating climate change and its impact on sustainability, gender issues, child labor, health, and many other real-life learning experiences that encouraged them to take action. The PYP changed how students and teachers reacted to their world. Teachers learned how to change their behavior for the betterment of themselves, the program, and their students. Teachers and students became inquirers, expressing that they would find it difficult if they had to transition to a non-IB school. As a leader, I was encouraged by those who believed in the vision. We had changed the mindset, allowing individual teachers to recognize that progressive teaching and learning were beneficial for all.

Suzette's story highlights the power of mentorship. As gatekeepers and cheerleaders, mentors can help illuminate what might otherwise be a very uncertain pathway for women into leadership. Though her early career was marked by hard work and persistence, it was her commitment to having integrity, being open-minded, and leading with heart that paved Suzette's path to educational leadership. She went from working all hours as a nurse and teacher to transforming her community by establishing the IB PYP. In this chapter, you'll look closely at the lessons Suzette learned and reflect on how these qualities inform your experiences as a leader.

Leadership Lessons

Suzette understood that any change she made as a leader would heighten emotions within her organization. Suzette leveraged her connections and her ability to bring different opinions together. She created an environment in which people understood that she cared deeply about the school community and the individuals who helped shape the school culture.

Having Integrity

Despite Suzette's passion for science, she was told early on that nursing was not for her. And while she found an equally compelling purpose in teaching, Suzette did not let go of the idea of being a nurse. When she decided to pursue both careers, she did so with tenacity. It took incredible strength and commitment to achieve, yet she believed in herself. Suzette is an example of what it looks like to strive for one's fullest potential, not to settle for *good enough*.

In his book *SOUL!,* mathematics educator and author Timothy D. Kanold (2021) writes about the role of integrity in what he calls an organization's *soul story*, the unique combination of core values and behaviors by which the organization defines itself:

> We model our moral and intellectual qualities, such as good judgment, best effort, respect, kindness, honesty, service, integrity, and citizenship. These virtues are modeled, upheld, and practiced in every part of our school's life for the benefit of the extended community.
>
> By ensuring our words, actions, and celebrations model positive behaviors for contributing to the greater good of our soul story, we refuse a mindset of "How good do we have to be for the community we serve to leave us alone, let us operate in isolation, and live our functional hypocrisy?"
>
> Instead, we earn the trust and respect of our extended community—every day, every school season, year in and year out—when we ask, "How good can we be?" (p. 171)

When they exhibit integrity, leaders foster trust among colleagues by demonstrating their commitment to moral and ethical behaviors and upholding their values even in the toughest seasons. Not only does this contribute to the success of the organization, but it also ripples out to the wider community.

REFLECTION QUESTIONS

Reflect on the following questions.

- In what ways and circumstances have you seen mentors or colleagues exhibiting integrity?

- How have you shown integrity in your own leadership experiences?

- In what ways do you wish to act with more integrity as a leader?

Being Open-Minded

Realizing that she could accomplish anything on which she set her sights, Suzette began to approach every challenge in life as an opportunity to grow. Over time, the relationships Suzette formed were the result of caring and openness, and these laid the foundation for her future successes. Suzette made a bold move to implement the IB PYP in her school, an initiative that would not have been possible without the collaboration of the close-knit team she'd cultivated.

Great school leaders are inquisitive and use open-ended questions to learn about their staff and build robust relationships. They strive to create a culture of trust where team members are encouraged to speak up. Associate professor Zhike Lei (2017) explains how a leader's open-mindedness empowers colleagues to amplify warning signs without fear of punishment:

> Leaders need to create "voice" opportunities by asking thoughtful questions, explicitly inviting employees' inputs, and listening actively and intensively. When a leader exhibits a supportive style and open-mindedness for deviant opinions, employees are motivated to speak up and amplify the weak signals.

Leaders challenge their employees to think critically and identify threats to the organization. Ultimately, leaders are responsible for responding to opportunities and threats, but by having an open-door policy, they invite the support of their colleagues.

REFLECTION QUESTIONS

Reflect on the following questions.

- Why is open-mindedness important? How can it help a leader?

- How have you seen open-mindedness as an asset in your leadership journey?

- In what ways do you strive to be more open-minded in relating to your colleagues?

Use figure 9.1 (page 118) to reflect on times you listened to others' insights to help you make a more informed decision, capture how your thinking changed when you considered someone else's view, and consider what lesson you learned from the experience.

Leading With Heart

Suzette allowed her profound belief that students are capable of great things to inform her work as a leader. She knew that the changes she was proposing would enable students to participate more meaningfully in the world. As a result, she was able to transmit the urgency of that message to those who could support that change. Though it wasn't the norm for an elementary school to initiate the IB PYP program, Suzette trusted her heart to guide her in doing what was best for students.

In *HEART! Fully Forming Your Professional Life as a Teacher and Leader*, Kanold (2017) presents the concept of a *heartprint*—the distinct impression that educators' hearts leave on students and colleagues during their professional career. Kanold (2017) writes that great teaching and leading are a form of love: "Great teachers and leaders see beyond your predisposed rough edges. They open you up—your mind and your heart—to a world of learning and new meaning. They teach you with a *whole heart*" (pp. 19–20). A leader who loves their work, their colleagues, and their organization leaves a powerful mark upon them. By having the courage to lead with their heart, they build an enduring legacy.

REFLECTION QUESTIONS

Reflect on the following questions.

- What is the distinctive heartprint you leave on students and colleagues?
- How has following your heart allowed you to exert a positive influence within your organization?
- What is one way you'd like to grow in your ability to lead with your heart?

Food for Thought

Becky Bermont is vice president of Media + Partners for the Rhode Island School of Design (RISD). Bermont (2009) wrote an article in the *Harvard Business Review* in which she notes that strong leaders invite tough questions. Suzette exhibited this trait in her commitment to question how and why decisions are made. Bermont (2009) calls this ability *critical leading*: a living, working critique on leadership. Many of the questions we ask do not have easily apparent answers. Especially when it comes to making

List an example of a time when embracing others' insights helped you make a more informed decision.	
How did your thinking change by considering someone else's view?	
What lesson will you carry with you as a result?	

FIGURE 9.1: Worksheet for teasing out open-mindedness.

Visit go.SolutionTree.com/leadership for a free reproducible version of this figure.

decisions in the creative sphere—like whether to push forward with an experimental initiative like the program Suzette implemented—leaders must take intuitive leaps rather than incremental steps.

When Suzette led her school through the IB process, she was clear with her intention and walked alongside her board, leaders, and employees to show them the way. Her transparency around her decision making helped build trust among her staff.

Conclusion

Suzette led with her heart, showed an open mind in her decision making, and acted with integrity. The art of diplomacy (or tact) can be a deciding factor between hurt feelings and a positive encounter, both in the workplace and beyond. Educational leaders must strive to maintain honesty at all times and should seek to convey information to colleagues, superiors, and subordinates in a clear and compassionate manner. Fred Coon, CEO of Stewart, Cooper & Coon (n.d.), writes that "diplomacy strengthens relationships in the workplace by decreasing the level of negative emotional impact upon the delivery of unfavorable news or feedback." When it comes to any negotiation, with a teacher, a parent, or a supervisor, tact and diplomacy are invaluable. Suzette's story illustrates the remarkable possibilities of such heart-centered leadership. Leaders must strive to be compassionate, kindhearted, and sincere if they wish to maintain strong and productive relationships with their colleagues and stakeholders.

SUZETTE'S LEADERSHIP LESSONS

Having integrity

Being open-minded

Leading with heart

References and Resources

Alaba, S. (2017). *The art of leadership and diplomacy*. Accessed at https://moderndiplomacy .eu/2017/10/26/the-art-of-leadership-and-diplomacy on July 19, 2021.

Bermont, B. (2009, October 21). Asking questions about transparency. *Harvard Business Review*. Accessed at https://hbr.org/2009/10/asking-questions-about-transpa on July 19, 2021.

Chandler, A. (2017, April 17). *Smart review:* HEART! Fully Forming Your Professional Life as a Teacher and Leader. Accessed at www.gettingsmart.com/2017/04/smart -review-heart-fully-forming-your-professional-life-as-a-teacher-and-leader on July 19, 2021.

Coon, F. (n.d.). *The importance of diplomacy in the workplace and how to achieve it* [Blog post]. Accessed at https://theusatwork.com/the-importance-of-diplomacy-in-the-workplace-and-how-to-achieve-it on August 12, 2021.

Hanson, J. (2006). *More than 85 broads: Women making career choices, taking risks, and defining success on their own terms.* New York: McGraw Hill.

Kanold, T. D. (2017). *HEART! Fully forming your professional life as a teacher and leader.* Bloomington, IN: Solution Tree Press.

Kanold, T. D. (2021). *SOUL! Fulfilling the promise of your professional life as a teacher and leader.* Bloomington, IN: Solution Tree Press.

Lei, Z. (2017). Thriving through crisis: A resiliencing approach. *Graziadio Business Review, 20*(2). Accessed at https://gbr.pepperdine.edu/2017/08/thriving-through-crisis-a-resiliencing-approach on December 9, 2021.

CHAPTER 10

Bringing It All Together

*Leadership is about making others better
as a result of your presence and making sure
that impact lasts in your absence.*

—SHERYL SANDBERG

In this book, we have explored the leadership lessons of ten women, all education leaders in their own right, independent of their titles, degrees, or certifications. They have worked exceptionally hard, challenged limitations, been honest with themselves and others, and embraced the need to keep learning in their professional and personal lives. Pulling together the leadership lessons gleaned from the women in this book, we can easily identify five central threads that run through their stories of leadership: (1) self-awareness, (2) authenticity, (3) courage, (4) connectedness, and (5) resilience.

Leadership does not come easily. It is not a gift that one wakes up with one morning. It is not a magical potion that one can take, instantly changing life's course. It comes with great risk and sometimes at great cost. And yet, those who become leaders will always find in that cost a silver lining. They have the capacity to humbly reflect and to try again, moving next time in the direction of a different outcome. Leaders are impassioned, they believe in their purpose, and they have faith in a future they cannot necessarily see. Even though the stories of Kate McKenna, Elsa Donohue, Michelle Kuhns, Debra Lane, Kimberly Cullen, Aleasha Morris, Pauline O'Brien, Francesca Mulazzi, Maya Nelson, and Suzette Julien are all different, the themes are familiar. While their stories illustrate a range of qualities that leaders may exhibit, each of these ten leaders exhibits all five of these characteristics to varying degrees. Women who strive to be successful leaders should develop these five key characteristics.

In this final chapter, you will explore each of the five characteristics more deeply, engaging with exercises and exploring resources to support your professional growth.

Self-Awareness

Because success means different things to different people, it does not have a universal definition that guides everyone's actions and decisions. Success for Elsa looked different than it did for Aleasha. For Elsa, it meant doing what she felt was most meaningful, leading the charge in a school and facing the greatest challenges with grace and serenity. For Aleasha, success meant finding a way to help people, not as the leader of a school per se, but independently as a coach, working to lift people into the best possible versions of themselves.

A starting point for anyone seeking success is to understand what kind of success it is that they seek. That is to say, it's necessary to be self-aware. When we're pointing to this innate understanding of one's highest values and most meaningful path, we're really talking about self-awareness, "the ability to see yourself clearly and objectively through reflection and introspection" (Ackerman, 2021).

The stories you've read throughout the book illustrated how a leader's ability to inspire and move people comes from her understanding of who she is, what she wants from the universe, and what she wishes to give to it.

The path of self-awareness is not always an easy one. Practicing self-awareness will require you to ask difficult questions, such as the following.

> What do I see as my strengths?

> What do others see as my strengths?

> What do I feel I need help with?

> What do others feel I need help with?

> How can I reconcile any differences between perception and reality?

> Who do I want to be? Who am I now?

> Where have I been and how does that contribute to where I am now?

> What am I okay with?

> What am I not okay with?

> What boundaries do I need to develop?

> What are my biggest distractions?

For a woman educational leader, self-awareness means being honest with herself and accepting that she is vulnerable. It means having a profound belief in something she cannot see but can clearly imagine. Self-awareness requires you to identify the things that help you move in a positive direction but also those things that impede your progress. Being self-aware means committing to self-care, balance, faith in purpose, and ultimately, belief in yourself.

Exercises and Resources

Becoming conscious is a journey that most of us undertake in adulthood. And it's one we continue for a lifetime through committed action and dedicated practice. Where are you on that journey? Whether you're just beginning or you've had years of practice, you can benefit from incorporating the following exercises and resources into your life and work.

> **Assess your level of self-awareness:** Not sure where you are on the journey of self-awareness? Complete the Self Consciousness Scale (https://bit.ly/3CAXqaE; PositivePsychology.com, n.d.). This scale, created by Michael Scheier and Charles Carver (1985), has been validated and translated into several languages. It will help you to better understand the ideas you get stuck on and to shift instead to objective reflection.

> **Write a letter to you:** Practice self-compassion by writing a letter to yourself. Acknowledge mistakes you've made in the workplace (such as an unresolved conflict with a colleague or a decision that didn't have the expected outcome). Write about your regrets and embrace your feelings with compassion. Let yourself be human.

> **Discover your strengths:** Take the Values in Action Inventory (VIA) Character Strengths Survey (www.viacharacter.org). Knowing your character strengths and intentionally increasing them are important activities to build self-awareness.

Authenticity

In a world where leadership is a role that has been traditionally played by men, women have to adapt themselves to the expectations of that role or adapt the role to fit their unique strengths. In "The Power of Femininity," Virginia Zeringue (1997) discusses culturally valued masculine and feminine qualities. Traits that are traditionally considered to be masculine include: aggressive, ambitious, competitive, forceful, independent, individualistic, decisive, and self-sufficient, among others. Traditionally feminine qualities include: affectionate, soft-spoken, sympathetic, compassionate, gentle, tender, and understanding. In order to be successful in leadership, women have needed to exhibit more masculine traits. However, an aggressive man is socially more acceptable than an aggressive woman (Chernyak-Hai, Kim, & Tziner, 2018). Succeeding in leadership roles, then, has often been a double-edged sword. Women frequently become hardened to and by the challenges of leadership.

Despite the temptation to brace themselves for challenge by growing a thick skin, women must take the opposite approach—one of authenticity and vulnerability. In *The Gifts of Imperfection*, researcher and author Brené Brown (2010) writes, "Authenticity is the daily practice of letting go of who we think we're supposed to be and embracing who we are" (p. 50). Each of the women featured in this book has found a different way, their authentic way, to be successful. They have learned that in order to achieve their self-identified versions of success, they have to be true to themselves. For Kate (page 6), that meant being aware of how her identity as a woman might impact an audience. Her experiences taught her to embrace her identity, perhaps even addressing it right from the start.

Kate, Elsa, Michelle, Debra, Kimberly, Aleasha, Pauline, Francesca, Maya, and Suzette—each of these women recognized that a key factor of achieving a professional life worth living was to embrace and celebrate themselves for who they were.

Authenticity means being humble, acknowledging vulnerability, trusting yourself, and being willing to follow your own path, regardless of what others might expect of you. An authentic leader continually asks herself: Is this what I really think? Is this what I really want? Am I acting in a way that is aligned with my beliefs, my values, my goals? Am I living a meaningful life? Do I inspire trust in others?

Exercises and Resources

Embracing authenticity sounds noble, but it's not easy! Brown (2010) puts it so well: "most of us know that choosing authenticity in a culture that dictates everything from how much we're supposed to weigh to what our houses are supposed to look like is a huge undertaking" (p. 50). Like anything else, though, authenticity is built through practice. As you commit to practicing authenticity as a leader, look to the following exercises and resources to help you along the way.

> **Redefine your values:** To live an authentic life, you have to know what matters to you. Your values give rise to your decisions, priorities, and actions. What matters most to you in your life and your work? Finding your authentic self requires that you know what matters to you. Sit down in a quiet place with a journal and make a list of your professional values. Then brainstorm any practices or habits you need to adopt to live in greater alignment with those values.

> **Get creative with your introspection:** A great way to get to the bottom of your heart is to probe it for insight (teamsoul, 2018). Consider questions you may not spend much time thinking about. Use the following prompts to see yourself in a new light:

  • One resource I waste in my professional life

  • The trait I value most in others

  • One way I wish to improve my life but lack the courage to do so

  • The one thing that gets me down but shouldn't

> › **Know what brings you joy:** Relationship expert and master practitioner E. B. Johnson (2019) writes:

> *Being authentic means being in sync with who you really are, and it means being there for yourself and sticking up for yourself when the going gets tough. When you're authentic, you gain a higher sense of self-worth, a greater follow-through on goals and even boosted self-confidence and coping skills.*

> A great tool for getting in touch with what brings you joy is the "What Makes My Heart Sing?" exercise (https://bit.ly/31fJ5D7; The Coaching Tools Company, n.d.). This coaching tool, accessible for a small fee, can be powerful to help you get closer to your true needs.

Courage

So many aspects of a leader's role require her to possess courage. Perhaps most notable is that those we serve look to us to be decision makers, risk takers, and trailblazers. In "Differences That Make a Difference," Debra (Lane et al., 2021) shares her thoughts about why courage is essential for women educational leaders:

> *Courage comes from a place deep inside, where fear loses a battle against faith: faith in oneself and faith in the possibilities. Without this adherence to the knowledge that the outcome is more rewarding than the fear wants us to think it is, there would never be any reason to take risks. And women, who so often strive for perfection, who limit themselves for fear of not meeting up to the standard, for appearing weak, for not getting it right, will all too often convince themselves that the risk is not worth taking. Leadership appears in women who model courage.*

The women in this book have taken huge risks: moving to new countries, establishing boundaries, stepping outside of their comfort zones, defying externally imposed limits. They have challenged the norm, the status quo, traditional gender roles. They have applied for jobs, been rejected, and applied for more. They have continued to challenge themselves professionally while raising children. They have enrolled in doctoral studies. They have allowed themselves to be vulnerable. They have taken the high road. They have negotiated. They have understood when it was time to change.

Being courageous means being willing to fail; it means understanding that failure is really gain disguised as loss. Courage looks like asking yourself: *What is the worst thing that can happen? And if that happens, can I live with it? If I fail, how will I learn from this?* Courage means knowing yourself, being true to yourself, and understanding the sacrifices you are willing to make. Courage also requires optimism. Each woman, in her own way, believed that a leap of faith would bring something better, bigger, more meaningful for them and those they serve.

Exercises and Resources

Sometimes it seems like courage is a quality you're born with: you either have it, or you don't. But courage is like every other virtue: an ability that you build with practice and patience. In what ways do you already act with courage as a leader? In what ways do you want to grow your capacity for courageous action? Use the exercises and resources below to expand your practice of showing up courageously.

> **Learn to embrace failure:** In 2016, Princeton professor Johannes Haushofer shared a CV of his career failures on Twitter, and it went viral (*The Guardian*, 2016). Americans have a cultural obsession with the overnight success story and a pathological fear of failure. Haushofer's experience suggests that we all secretly know better. Failure is an inevitable and natural part of how humans grow and evolve. One way of flexing that courage muscle is to actively embrace failure. Big failures mean you had the courage to take big risks.
>
> Follow Haushofer's lead and make a list of your failures. Think back on each one, reflect on the lessons you learned along the way, and celebrate the growth that happened in the wake of those failures.

> **See it until you believe it:** Sports psychology frequently uses visualization to help athletes optimize performance, and sports medicine draws on the practice to help injured athletes recover. Director of athletics and adjunct professor Marty Durden (2017) explains, "If an athlete can first see it, then she can do it." One of the most powerful assets women leaders have is vision. They can visualize unique solutions or unlikely paths to achieving goals. Courage means trusting that vision. It means staying the course despite the roadblocks or criticism that tempts you to turn back. When self-doubt creeps in, you can draw on visualization as a tool for support.
>
> You can get started by practicing the Mental Rehearsal Technique Jack Canfield shares in the article "Visualization Techniques to Affirm Your Desired Outcomes: A Step-by-Step Guide" (https://bit.ly/3BqRjEu; Canfield, n.d.).

> **Complete a team-building exercise:** Team-building activities create cohesion between group members and promote problem solving. For this exercise, try the human knot (Li, 2020), a group activity that stretches a leader's ability to rely on others. Sometimes delegating a task, allowing our team to support us, and trusting in a colleague are the ultimate test of courage. To complete the human knot, gather six or more participants (you'll need an even number) and follow these instructions.

- Stand in a circle.

- Lock your right hand with someone across from you (avoid joining hands with the person beside you).

- Next, lock your left hand with someone across from you.

- Try to untangle yourselves without unlocking hands.

- For an extra challenge, establish a time limit for completing the exercise.

Connectedness

In his biography of Helen Keller, *Helen and Teacher*, journalist and author Joseph P. Lash (1980) records Helen's famous words: "Alone, we can do so little. Together, we can do so much" (p. 489). Leadership can sometimes feel like a lonely calling. Yet, connectedness is one of the themes repeated throughout this book. Each of the women in this book understood that they are not alone, that their success cannot be attributed solely to their own hard work. That is not to take away from the incredible effort each has made to be where she is today. Instead, these women have understood, with gratitude and appreciation, that they are the product of their community. Some referred to their parents and upbringing. Others talked extensively about the mentors who appeared in their lives along the way, challenging them to reach higher and dig deeper.

Connectedness requires humility and vulnerability. If leaders want to create connection, they must allow others in with grace and gratitude, knowing that they cannot succeed by themselves. In a Duke commencement speech, philanthropist Melinda Gates (2013) noted that "deep human connection . . . is the purpose and the result of a meaningful life—and it will inspire the most amazing acts of love, generosity, and humanity." Powerful, effective leaders know the value and necessity of connection. Connectedness teaches leaders to be empathetic, to care for others, and to seek understanding.

Connectedness involves cultural competence and acceptance of different views and perspectives. It allows leaders to ask: How can I reach others at a deeper level? What can I learn from this awkward or uncomfortable conversation? How will I grow from this relationship? What does this person need from me? Each woman's story illustrates that a person's willingness to know and be known is the hallmark of true connection.

Exercises and Resources

Think about the connections that define your day-to-day experience in the workplace. How connected do you feel to your coworkers? What practices, processes, and routines contribute to that experience? What barriers keep you from creating strong connections? Draw on the following exercises and resources to expand your sense of connectedness with your colleagues.

> **Write a gratitude letter:** Think back on a time when you felt deeply grateful to a colleague for something they did for you. Try to pick someone you currently work with, someone you could meet face-to-face in the next week.

Greater Good Science Center (n.d.a) suggests writing a letter to this person. Write directly to the person, describing what they taught you or how they contributed in some way to the leader you are today. If at all possible, deliver your letter in person. If you feel comfortable, you may even read the letter to them.

> **Remember your connections:** Being connected to others in your life doesn't happen by accident; it's a practice that you cultivate. Greater Good in Action (Greater Good Science Center, n.d.c), an initiative promoting research-based methods to help people thrive, offers an activity called Reminders of Connectedness. Use the following steps to complete the activity.

  - Look around your office. Notice the objects, patterns, images, and words that fill the space. How many of these items relate to social connectedness?

  - Notice empty spaces, walls, or shelves where you could add objects, images, or words that remind you of connectedness.

  - Seek out objects (purchase something, make a craft, or commission artwork) that evoke connection and place them in the empty spaces around the room.

> **Ask a trusted colleague for feedback:** Seeking feedback from a close team member is a vulnerable act. Vulnerability, active listening, and open-mindedness are essential ingredients of creating and fostering connections.

Resilience

Each woman's story told of a dream they were pursuing. That dream was not always clear, and sometimes they had to figure it out along the way. Sometimes achieving their dreams came about through trial and error. Making mistakes can be painful, but it's an inevitable part of becoming a successful leader. This is the power of resilience. It pushes leaders to keep going and reminds them that error is not the end, only a call to keep going, to keep growing.

In many ways, resilience is the pinnacle of leadership. Resilience is where we find each of the previous elements of leadership: self-awareness, authenticity, courage, and connectedness all give rise to resilience. Resilience brings all of the pieces together, resulting in a commitment to keep going. In resilience we find the best of grit, conviction, and determination. Leadership is about bringing people together to create, build, empower, connect, and change. None of those things are possible without facing down challenge. The women leaders in this book have each stood up to their share of obstacles, looked at them head on, and kept moving forward. The only way out is through.

Exercises and Resources

Resilience gives leaders the ability to rise to the occasion, to push through every obstacle, and to come out stronger, with an even greater capacity for leading others. Use the following exercises and resources to consider ways to bolster your resilience.

› **Let go of your anger:** Greater Good Science Center (n.d.b) suggests the following activity for finding compassion and letting go of anger.

   • Step 1—Find a quiet place to relax. Sit down and focus on your breath for two minutes. As you exhale, focus on the word "one."

   • Step 2—Identify a time when a parent, a staff member, or a student hurt or offended you.

   • Step 3—For the next two minutes think of this person as a human being who made a bad decision in how he, she, or they behaved. The relationship may not be restored; however, try to wish this person a positive interaction or healing. Allow yourself to move toward compassion. Become aware of your emotions and physical responses as you cultivate mercy for this person.

› **Reconnect to your inner self:** Life in our modern world is loud, busy, and highly distracting. With the internet and social media at our fingertips, our bodies can have a sense of always being geared up, ready to perform or respond to a question or meet a need at a moment's notice. That constant availability can leave us exhausted and at risk of burnout. To re-establish that connection with yourself and boost your inner reserves, practice stepping back and quieting the noise. It's okay to start small. Choose one of the following activities to practice once a week.

   • Spend time alone in nature.

   • Go for a leisurely walk.

   • Set all devices in another room and write in a journal.

   • Sit under the stars.

   • Watch the sunrise.

Notice how your body, mind, and heart respond to this space you create each week. Pay attention to your growing capacity to handle day-to-day challenges.

› **Practice self-compassion:** Jean Whitlock, Trinh Mai, Megan Call, and Jake Van Epps (2021), contributors to the online health initiative Accelerate, note that self-compassion increases well-being and resilience to stress and trauma as well as being linked to healthier behaviors, greater motivation, confidence, and a sense of personal responsibility. By taking a self-compassion break, you lean into building these healthier behaviors. This is something you can do any time you start to feel overwhelmed by pain or stress. Greater Good Science Center (n.d.d)

recommends a Self-Compassion Break (to access the full text, visit https://bit
.ly/3EoaBwi). Follow these steps to engage with this practice.

- Reflect on a situation that is difficult and is causing you stress.
- Get in touch with what happened or what you think might happen.
- Now say to yourself, "This is a moment of suffering."
- Next, say to yourself, "Suffering is a part of life."
- Now, put your hands over your heart, feel the warmth of your hands and notice the rhythm of your breath, and say, "May I be kind to myself."

Each woman's path to educational leadership is unique. And yet, all great leaders possess the five characteristics we've examined: (1) self-awareness, (2) authenticity, (3) courage, (4) connectedness, and (5) resilience. As you engage with the exercises and resources in this chapter, you'll be investing in yourself, your colleagues, and your organization.

References and Resources

Ackerman, C. E. (2021, June 12). *What is self-awareness and why is it important? [+5 ways to increase it]*. Accessed at https://positivepsychology.com/self-awareness-matters -how-you-can-be-more-self-aware/ on December 9, 2021.

Branden, N. (1995). *The six pillars of self-esteem: The definitive work on self-esteem by the leading pioneer in the field*. New York: Bantam.

Brown, B. (2010). *The gifts of imperfection: Let go of who you think you're supposed to be and embrace who you are*. Center City, MN: Hazelden.

Canfield, J. (n.d.). *Visualization techniques to affirm your desired outcomes: A step-by-step guide*. Accessed at www.jackcanfield.com/blog/visualize-and-affirm-your-desired -outcomes-a-step-by-step-guide/ on July 19, 2021.

Chernyak-Hai, L., Kim, S.-K., & Tziner, A. (2018). Gender profiles of workplace individual and organizational deviance. *Journal of Work and Organizational Psychology, 34*(1), 46–55.

The Coaching Tools Company. (n.d.). *What makes my heart sing? exercise*. Accessed at www.thecoachingtoolscompany.com/products/what-makes-my-heart-sing on July 19, 2021.

Durden, M. (2017). Utilizing imagery to enhance injury rehabilitation. *The Sport Journal, 19*, 1–5. Accessed at https://thesportjournal.org/article/utilizing-imagery -to-enhance-injury-rehabilitation/ on February 11, 2022.

Etukuru, R. R. (2018). *The art and science of transformational leadership: Unleashing creativity, innovation, and leadership to embrace transformative change*. Bloomington, IN: iUniverse.

Gates, M. (2013). *Duke commencement 2013.* Accessed at www.gatesfoundation.org/ideas /speeches/2013/05/melinda-gates-duke-commencement-2013 on July 19, 2021.

Greater Good Science Center. (n.d.a). *Gratitude letter.* Accessed at https://ggia.berkeley .edu/practice/gratitude_letter on October 28, 2021.

Greater Good Science Center. (n.d.b). *Letting go of anger through compassion.* Accessed at https://ggia.berkeley.edu/practice/letting_go_of_anger_through_compassion on October 28, 2021.

Greater Good Science Center. (n.d.c). *Reminders of connectedness.* Accessed at https:// ggia.berkeley.edu/practice/reminders_of_connectedness on July 15, 2021.

Greater Good Science Center. (n.d.d). *Self-compassion break.* Accessed at https://ggia .berkeley.edu/practice/self_compassion_break on August 17, 2021.

The Guardian. (2016). *CV of failures: Princeton professor publishes resume of his career lows.* Accessed at www.theguardian.com/education/2016/apr/30/cv-of-failures -princeton-professor-publishes-resume-of-his-career-lows on August 16, 2021.

Johnson, E. B. (2019). *Start being authentic if you want to find joy in this life.* Accessed at https://medium.com/lady-vivra/how-to-live-authentically-85112bd434bc on August 13, 2021.

Lane, D., Lockwood, J., Luce, A. M., McNamer, B., Mulazzi, F., & Prendergast, L. (2021, May 10). *Differences that make a difference: Stories & strategies to inspire women leaders.* Accessed at www.ecis.org/stories_strategies_inspire_women_leaders on December 9, 2021.

Lash, J. P. (1980). *Helen and teacher.* New York: Random House.

Li, L. (2020, June 1). *20 team building activities to build trust among coworkers.* Accessed at www.tinypulse.com/blog/team-building-activity-trust on December 9, 2021.

Miller, K. (2021, May 31). *Building self-awareness: 16 activities and tools for meaningful change.* Accessed at https://positivepsychology.com/building-self-awareness -activities/ on October 28, 2021.

Moioli, F. (2020). *Our ikigai is different for all of us, but one thing we have in common is that we are all searching for meaning.* Accessed at www.linkedin.com/pulse/our-ikigai -different-all-us-one-thing-we-have-common-searching-fabio on August 17, 2021.

Neff, K. (2018). *Guided self-compassion meditations.* Accessed at www.self-compassion .org/guided-self-compassion-meditations-mp3–2 on July 19, 2021.

PositivePsychology.com. (n.d.). *Self-consciousness scale.* Accessed at https://positivepsychology .com/wp-content/uploads/Self-Consciousness-Scale.pdf on July 19, 2021.

Scheier, M. F., & Carver, C. S. (1985). The self-consciousness scale: A revised version for use with general populations. *Journal of Applied Social Psychology, 15*(8), 687–699. Accessed at https://onlinelibrary.wiley.com/doi/abs/10.1111/j.1559 -1816.1985.tb02268.x on July 19, 2021.

teamsoul. (2018, January 9). *5 keys to finding your authentic self and shedding your mask.* Accessed at https://iamfearlesssoul.com/finding-your-authentic-self on October 28, 2021.

Whitlock, J., Mai, T., Call, M., & Van Epps, J. (2021, February 4). *How to practice self-compassion for resilience and well-being.* Accessed at https://accelerate.uofuhealth.utah.edu/resilience/how-to-practice-self-compassion-for-resilience-and-well-being on August 17, 2021.

Zeringue, V. (1997). *The power of femininity: An examination of the qualities women in leadership possess.* Senior thesis project, University of Tennessee, Knoxville. Accessed at https://trace.tennessee.edu/cgi/viewcontent.cgi?article=1026&context=utk_interstp2 on July 19, 2021.

Epilogue

KIMBERLY CULLEN

It takes a lot of courage to share your story with an invisible audience. You can't interpret your reader's expression, and you can't be sure that the words you have so carefully chosen are being read in the same tone that you imagined when you wrote them. Writing is a daunting process, and it becomes that much scarier when you're writing about your own vulnerabilities.

We want to thank our contributors for opening their hearts and minds to an invisible audience and for trusting in Debra and me to give their stories the thoughtful prominence they deserved. When we began this project, we didn't know exactly where the work would lead us. We couldn't guarantee the final product or that there would even be a final product. When you decide to write a book, you are essentially jumping off a cliff, hoping that the parachute will deploy in time. Aleasha, Michelle, Suzette, Kate, Maya, Francesca, Elsa, and Pauline: you were our parachutes. We are so grateful for your strength, your persistence, your willingness to give voice to the challenges and victories that women experience on the path to leadership.

Significant advancements are being made in the movement toward global gender parity. To see that women are less afraid to speak up against the injustices of sexual harassment and rape culture, that women are striking the word *female* from their own self-descriptions (for example, "~~female~~ CEO," "~~female~~ head of school"), and that research increasingly celebrates the effectiveness of women leadership in crisis, as was the case throughout the pandemic in 2020, gives us great hope that maybe, just maybe, we won't have to wait 208 years for things to equal out.

Debra and I continue to work actively with women educators—both those in leadership and those who aspire to leadership. We know firsthand how difficult it can be to overcome barriers outside of our making, and we believe that the real key to moving parity forward is helping people uncover their potential. As educators, we believe it is the responsibility of every single person in a position of influence to lift others up. Everyone, independent of gender, can do this work.

Our book highlights the stories of ten women, but there are so many more. Everyone has a story. We hope that you will be inspired to listen to those around you, to ask questions with the goal of understanding, and to do your part to personally make a difference, not only for others but also for yourself. By now, we hope you will have identified specific ways that you can:

> ➤ Transform your leadership practice into one that is more collaborative, research-based, and effective

> ➤ Understand where you can start making changes that will help foster growth in your learning community

> ➤ Provide more stakeholders with a voice in your community

> ➤ Invite a variety of constituents and mentors into your leadership plan and exercises

> ➤ Empower women to help one another become successful educational leaders

> ➤ *Raise her up!*

Index

Step In, Step Up
Jane A. G. Kise and Barbara K. Watterston
Step In, Step Up guides current and aspiring women leaders in education through a twelve-week development journey. An assortment of activities, reflection prompts, and stories empowers readers to overcome gender barriers and engage in opportunities to learn, grow, and lead within their school communities.
BKF827

The Deliberate and Courageous Principal
Rhonda J. Roos
Fully step into your power as a school principal. By diving deep into five essential leadership _actions_ and five essential leadership _skills_, you will learn how to grow in your role and accomplish incredible outcomes for your students and staff.
BKG013

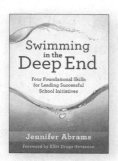

Swimming in the Deep End
Jennifer Abrams
Acquire the knowledge and resources necessary to lead successful change initiatives in schools. In _Swimming in the Deep End_, author Jennifer Abrams dives deep into the four foundational skills required of effective leadership and provides ample guidance for cultivating each.
BKF830

180 Days of Self-Care for Busy Educators
Tina H. Boogren
Rely on _180 Days of Self-Care for Busy Educators_ to help you lead a happier, healthier, more fulfilled life inside and outside of the classroom. With Tina H. Boogren's guidance, you will work through 36 weeks of self-care strategies during the school year.
BKF920